Simon Somerville Laurie

**Institutes of Education**

Comprising an introduction to rational psychology

Simon Somerville Laurie

**Institutes of Education**
*Comprising an introduction to rational psychology*

ISBN/EAN: 9783744751957

Printed in Europe, USA, Canada, Australia, Japan

Cover: Foto ©Suzi / pixelio.de

More available books at **www.hansebooks.com**

# INSTITUTES OF EDUCATION

# INSTITUTES OF EDUCATION

COMPRISING AN

## INTRODUCTION TO RATIONAL PSYCHOLOGY

*DESIGNED (PARTLY) AS A TEXT-BOOK FOR
UNIVERSITIES AND COLLEGES*

BY

## S. S. LAURIE, M.A., LL.D.

PROFESSOR OF THE INSTITUTES AND HISTORY OF EDUCATION
IN THE UNIVERSITY OF EDINBURGH

New York
MACMILLAN AND CO,
AND LONDON
1892

# PREFACE.

I BEGAN this book as a Handbook for the students of my own class. It grew in the course of production. I felt that I could be of most service to students, and perhaps also to Lecturers on Education, if I printed in full the more abstract portions of my argument — those, namely, which dealt with the philosophy of method. The result is that the volume is more than a Handbook and less than a Treatise.

I have used the term on the title-page, "rational psychology," to distinguish my point of view. Doubtless it might be maintained that no one should in these days attempt any philosophy of mind until empirical psychology has completed its microscopic task, and psycho-physics has said its last word. This would be to strike dumb all but the devotees of physical experimentation, while they themselves do not hesitate to travel outside their peculiar field, and commit themselves to speculative opinions (*e.g.* freedom of the Will) which contain implicit in them a whole metaphysical system. It will be granted that the uncorrelated phenomena of consciousness, which empirical psychology offers us, cannot in itself yield a theory of knowledge, much less a philosophy of life. There must be some principle, idea (call it what you will), which correlates and unifies. And until that principle emerges out of the laboratory (if that is to be its birthplace), we may be allowed our own thoughts as to its probable whereabouts. In any case a writer on the theory of Education is really writing at once a theory of life and a treatise *De emendatione intellectus,* and he cannot dispense with a rational and rationalised scheme of mind, be it right or wrong. He will be thankful for all that physiology and physics can give him; but meanwhile, and until better advised, he must follow his own course. What I have to say is a practical application of my books on Metaphysics and Ethics.

After all, psycho-physics can never be *more than physics,* though it may throw some light on the characteristics, as well as the conditions, of sensational elements.

The notes at the end of some of the lectures, and the whole of the Appendix, are to be omitted by students of Education. They are written chiefly for my own satisfaction, to justify and supplement the text; but they are not needed for the understanding of it. To the general student of philosophy they may be interesting.

It is quite unnecessary, in my opinion, to carry students of Education into all the details of Logic, Psychology, Ethics, and Physiology. It is necessary, however, that the philosophy which they study should be seen to be truly the Science of the Art. Accordingly, students have to get a firm hold, by the help of their instructors, of the fundamental principles which exhibit the nature and growth of mind. Everything which diverts their attention from this is useless, so far as the science and art of Education are concerned.

S. S. LAURIE.

University of Edinburgh,
*October* 1892.

# TABLE OF CONTENTS.

## PART I.

### THE END, PHYSIOLOGICAL CONDITIONS, MATERIALS, AND METHOD OF EDUCATION GENERALLY.

## PART II.

vii

## PART III.

## PART IV.

## PART V.

(*Nutrition and Discipline: Real and Formal.*)

# PART VI.

# PART VII.

# PART I.

*THE END, PHYSIOLOGICAL CONDITIONS,
MATERIALS, AND METHOD OF
EDUCATION GENERALLY.*

# INTRODUCTION.

## EDUCATIONAL LIMITATIONS AND POSSIBILITIES.

/5/05

ENTHUSIASTS have spoken as if we could manufacture men after a certain pattern, if only we proceeded wisely. Religious and educational reformers have often cherished this belief. It is as well to set aside such pious dreams at once. Conditions outside our activity as educators are too potent. We have to reckon with all the forces that make for or against us —instincts, passions, custom, connate predispositions, and racial characteristics.

Locke, with all his sobriety of temperament, yet held that the difference between one man and another lay in their education. Even if we take education in its widest sense, as including all the influences at work from infancy upwards, Locke's view would be incorrect; if we take it in its narrower sense of the conscious and regulated education of the school and family, it is altogether untenable. If, however, we understand Locke to mean by education the bringing up of a human being so as to fit him for ordinary citizenship, and make him a respectable member of society and a satisfactory representative of the moral standard and social consensus of his time, he is unquestionably right. We can do even more than this;

1

for we can train youth to something higher and better than the "spirit of the age."

The question did not escape the attention of the ancients. Horace says —

"Naturam expellas furca tamenusque recurret."

He is right, for we cannot overpower entirely the determinations of nature in each man. But he is also right when he says —

"Nemo adeo ferus est ut non mitescere possit,
   Si modo culturæ patientem commodet aurem,"

which amounts to this, that however strong a natural disposition to wrong may be, it can be largely modified, if not wholly extirpated, by education. Juvenal, as becomes his *rôle* of truculent satirist, takes a gloomy view of human nature and its possibilities. Seneca the Stoic, again, thinks that much may be done if we begin early, but has no hope of those who are allowed to reach maturity with their faults and vices uncorrected. It is then too late. "As the twig is bent, the tree is inclined." He also thinks that education never wholly eradicates a vice or failing, but only modifies it. Plato says that man is the most savage of all animals, but that he can be made the gentlest and most godlike by education, if there be a good disposition in him; meaning by disposition, I imagine, such a general tendency of nature as gives a hopeful field for cultivation. Quintilian substantially takes the same view; but he believes more in the power of education, as such, than Plato does. Plato's hope lay not in the school so much as in the whole social organisation. Then there is the Greek proverb, which in its Latin form seems to be approved by Erasmus, "Non quovis ex ligno fit Mercurius," which may be paralleled by the form in which an aged Scotch educationalist used to throw the conclusion to which he had come in dealing with the vigorous but rough and often coarse-grained Scottish youth, "You can never put the polish of marble on a bit of sandstone."

Modern enthusiasts have, as a rule, been much more sanguine than the ancient critics of humanity. Comenius, for example, had a firm conviction that by education all men might be made perfect. Cicero perhaps best sums up ancient opinion and the conclusion of common sense, "Quæ bona sunt fieri meliora possunt doctrina, et quæ non optima aliquo modo acui tamen et corrigi possunt."

We may safely hold that, save in exceptional cases which may be regarded as abnormal products, education wisely directed can form men into good citizens if we begin the process of formation early; that is to say, it can guarantee in all, that amount of intelligence and virtue and that standard of social intercourse which fit them to discharge well the ordinary duties of men in all their political, industrial, and personal relations. But when we go beyond this and strive to bring all men up to an ideal standard, either of intellectual capacity or moral elevation, we are largely dependent on the original and connate potentialities of each, and we shall fail or succeed according as we have the natural tendency on our side or against us.

The greatest genius has defects, both of intelligence and character, which education will do much to remove; but whatever the education, genius will "out" in some form or other. The man of moderate genius, on the other hand, is almost wholly dependent on education for the growth of such powers as he has. Still more is this the case with the "average man." Those again who are by nature distinctly below the average can by education be brought up to the average, and help to swell the social current which already tends in its main stream to good. The lowest natures, finally, — the residuum, — are held in check by those above them, and can and must be disciplined, by the help of the whip, to obey their betters for the common good.

I am speaking, however, of education in the large sense, and as comprehending all the influences of a man's environment as he grows from childhood to maturity. The most potent of these is the home; next in potency comes the modern school, when its function is properly understood.

The school is the schoolmaster, just as the family is the parent.

As to the School:

Whatever may be the natural tendencies and capacities of each child, all can be made better by education than they would otherwise be, and all have, by virtue of their possession of reason, a certain ideal of life growing in them, which can be further elevated and confirmed by the teacher who puts before himself an ideal aim. There is, in every age, a conception of ideal manhood; and to this and for this we all must work in the field of education, if we are to work to any good purpose. By striving to reach the top, as Quintilian says, we get higher up than by sitting down despairingly at the bottom of the hill. The aim of education is, in truth, always an ideal aim, for it contemplates the completion of a man, — the realisation in each man of what each has it in him to become. If a teacher has not an. ideal aim he had better take to shopkeeping at once; he will there, doubtless, find an ideal within his capacity.

In his necessary ignorance of the possibilities of each individual, the educator is justified in taking up his task on the assumption that every member of the human race is, by virtue of his distinctive humanity, endowed with the same general capacities and powers, and has in him the possibility of a *complete* development. This is the assumption of his science and art. He does not recognise a qualitative difference in human beings, but merely a quantitative. No doubt, with all men the possible development is "thus far and no farther." The limitations as determined by physical constitution, by locality, by race, and by heredity, must be theoretically admitted; but they may be practically ignored. The aim of the educator is determined by his conception of the ideal man, towards which all may, more or less, be disciplined and trained.

The influences which educate a man (as I have already indicated) are both vast and subtle, the na-

tional tradition, the family life, the unconscious pressure of law and custom, the solicitations of external
nature, and all the local circumstances peculiar to the
environment of each.   These, however, are fully admitted by the rational educationalist; but he at the
same time claims to supplement, to regulate and control, the various and manifold influences at work, so as
to harmonise the varied experience of the young into a
rational unity of life and character, and thus get them
within sight at least of the ideal possible for each.

The intelligent teacher will also recognise that the
natural educators are the parents, and that they are
always the most potent for good or evil.  But, as the
exigencies of modern society have deputed much of
the parental work to a special order in the State, he
will also recognise that he, as a member of that order,
has great responsibilities, and is under obligation to
study education with a view to the proper discharge
of these.   His function is, probably, the most important of all social functions.

The duty of a professor of education is, I think, to
give the students of the subject an ideal and also a
method; but, above all, to inspire them with a sense
of the infinite importance and delicacy of their task.
He has to show them that they are not mere exactors
of lessons, but trainers of the human spirit ; and also
*how*, animated by this larger conception, they may,
in teaching subjects, educate minds.   He will expose
the popular fallacy that the schoolmaster's work is
a drudgery, and convince his students that it is a privilege.

# LECTURE I.

THE word "Education" does not mean drawing out.
This is a modern gloss on the true meaning of the
word—a gloss suggested by psychology. It means
training up, as vines are trained up poles. The primary signification of a word is not always a safe guide
to its present use, though it is always interesting and
suggestive. When men first name a thing or process,
there often, perhaps generally, precedes the naming
(always a work of unconscious genius) a flash of
insight into the essential character of the thing or
process named. The Latin conception of education
is confirmed by our own early usage of the word, *e.g.*
"Train up a child in the way he should go," and by
the German *erziehen*.

Train up, draw up, not draw *out*—is the meaning of
the word "educate," and it is a name for the process
which we cannot, I think, supersede without loss.

Train up to what? Evidently to some end or other.
To what end? Looking at the nature of man, we
answer, To some habit of being and doing which the
child knows nothing of, but which we, the trainers,
are supposed to have as our aim, and of which every
child is held to be capable.

7

What, then, is *your* aim? You cannot define it closely, nor even describe it, when the question is first put to you; but, all the same, there is vaguely in your mind some type of manhood or womanhood up to which you yourself are striving to live, and to which, if you are in earnest, you desire to train the young. This type you have more or less consciously present to your mind, and you call it your "ideal."

Now, the mass of men and women, even including parents, may be left to an ideal which is floating and vague; but it is the business and the duty of all who adopt what is called the "profession" of education, to have some clear conception of the ideal up to which they train — a conscious end, which they can express in words. It is, when you think of it, a very daring thing in you to profess to educate a human being. Where are your credentials? It seems to me that one who stands before the world and professes to educate is guilty of an impertinence, unless he can produce a commission, not from an university or a college, but from God Himself. It is a grave and serious business. In any case, it is surely not too much to demand of you that you have some definite ideal. Why, a cabinetmaker has his ideal of the completed cabinet, as he saws and cuts, planes and joints and polishes. You are engaged in forming the finest, most complex, most subtle thing known to man, viz. a mind; and do you propose to go on from day to day as your fancy prompts, tinkering here and tinkering there, and seeing what comes of it? Surely not.

Now, I wish next to say that the ideal you have for

those whom you educate must be the ideal you have
for yourself — your own life. You cannot rise above
yourself, any more than you can carry your head in
your mouth. This is the true meaning of the saying,
"As is the teacher, so is the school," to which I beg
you to add an even more important truth, "As is the
man, so is the teacher." The prime qualification,
then, in the teacher who educates, is that he shall
have an ideal for his own life, and shall be educating
*himself* up to that : your pupils learn by doing what
you do. The educator has first of all to look to himself, and the study of education is also the education
of the student: the ideal and method are for him first,
and for his pupils next.

Whatever ideal he may have for himself as a
human being, and consequently for his pupils, the
teacher may depend on this, that the young cannot
form abstract ideals as he does : they look to the
parent or teacher as the concrete embodiment of that
which they are to strive to be. You may inculcate
what you please, but all the time you yourself as a
personality are doing more than all your inculcations
can do. This is a common-place. Very few parents
and teachers have had conscious ideals ; but, as I have
indicated, there is an unconscious ideal in every man's
bosom which moulds his character and governs his
actions, or at least prescribes what *ought* to govern.

The early history of education is, like the history
of other subjects, a history, not of conscious and formulated ends, ideals, and processes, but of the unconscious ends pursued by nations as they advanced from

barbarism to civilisation, and to the fulfilment of their destiny in the world-history. These unconscious ends are merely vague feelings of a result to be aimed at rather than a distinct knowledge of it, and yet they are most potent: they make history. As age succeeds age, the ideal becomes gradually more explicit. Society begins to propose to itself specific aims, that is to say, the development of certain definite faculties which it desires to see active in all its citizens. Vigour of body, courage, endurance, skill in the use of arms, skill in this or that industry, obedience to civil law, and so forth: all excellent in their way, but neither singly nor in the aggregate an ideal of man as a living spirit in a living body — a being of vast and varied capacity, of rich possibilities, and whose life and acts have infinite issues. Such an ideal as this we first have among the Greeks, and thereafter more fully in Christianity. Man as man, man for the sake of man, not for his skill in doing this or that — this is, since the days of Plato and Christ, the aim of the educator. Not what man is, but what he may be in all his relations, finite and infinite — this is the problem of the educational ideal.

I would, however, beg you not to suppose that education was invented either by the Greek or the Christian world. It has always been going on. Every child, always, at all times, and in all places, is being educated — trained up to something or other which constitutes the type for his time, his place, or his class. The reflective movement in education, beginning, perhaps, with Plato, is simply part of the philosophy of man, and therefore is to be justified as all philosophy is to be justified. Philosophy in its ultimate meaning is nothing but persistent thought on man, his nature, his capabilities, his purpose, and his destiny. And the philosophy of education is simply the asking and answering of questions as to the ends or ideals of the philosophy of man, criticising custom in the light of these, and then studying the processes by which true ends can be best reached — *i.e.* Method.

In all ages of the world man has been educated: not only so, but I would say further, that we cannot afford to despise the education of early races; at least, when men had reached the stage of settled agricultural communities. In those primitive days you can easily see that the education would be mainly what is now called technical; that is to say, such instruction as fitted the young as they grew up to supply their daily bodily wants. Difficulties of communication, the rudimentary state of the useful arts, the dangers and uncertainties to which individuals would be exposed in maintaining intercourse with each other, would prevent the division of labour and the growth of that industrial interdependence which is now an universal characteristic of civilised life. This state of things, which gave a narrow horizon to each, had its educational compensations; for each man, with the help of his household, would be himself master of many, if not of all, necessary arts. From childhood upwards he would be in continual training to these. We should accordingly err much were we to despise the education of those primitive times. We still find it in many parts of the world, and survivals of it even in our own land. The family which not only milked its own cows, made its own butter and cheese, and ground its own corn, but clipped its own sheep, cleaned, combed, dyed, and spun the wool, and then wove it into cloth and made it into clothes; which prepared its own cow-hides for the feet or the target, which made its own rude articles of furniture and moulded its own pottery, — had no small skill. The faculties were by these occupations trained, and popular instruction might be said to be universal and domestic. There was more than instruction in those prehistoric days, there was "training up" to a certain standard of effectiveness in the work of life; and there was, besides, provision for a higher life, although the literature might be limited to the chanting of a few rude ballads, indulgence in rustic mimes, and the worship of a god or gods which were merely tribal.

Were we now, in these modern times, to educate a man merely with a view to the adaptation of his powers to certain finite uses (industries and the like), we should be recurring to the education of primeval civilisation without the advantages of our remote ancestors. For there is now a minute division of labour in industries, and the breadth and variety of primitive technical education is gone for ever. If, as a substitute for breadth, we were to train a man (as in modern times we can do) to a knowledge of those principles which should regulate the application of his powers to the narrow field of his industrial work,

we, while undoubtedly calling into activity his reason, would yet be doing so with definite and restricted
reference to mere finite and bodily uses. This would be
a decided advance on mere training of the practical
powers in accordance with custom; but it would not be
education, but only what we now understand by technical instruction. We should be putting brains into a
man's fingers; but this is not, I repeat, education,
though it contributes to it. It falls far short even of
the education of the primitive settler; it gains in ra-
tionality, but it loses in variety and breadth, and in
its demand on the power of men to meet exigencies.

When we speak of educating a human being, we
think of something more than this. We all think of
more than this when we think of the subject at all.
There is (as I have before indicated) a presupposition underlying our conception of the word education.
That presupposition will be found to be this — that in
man, unlike the animals, there are the germs of a
possible growth to something or other to which we
cannot set limits; and this something or other is our
ideal. So long as we keep this in view we are giving
a "liberal," as opposed to a "technical" education.
It is the recognition of this potentiality in man which
makes us strive to educate youth and to educate ourselves. A man is not a mere intelligent tool; he is
something more. He exists for that something more.
He is not a means but an end. A material civilisation is to be called civilisation only in so far as it
makes the higher end possible for a community. We
begin to see, in fact, that the education of man up to

a certain ideal is itself the very purpose of his existence, and that the history of our race is, properly
viewed, the history of its education.

Education, however, in this larger sense was not in
old times possible. For this reason: by education,
we mean the training of a man with a view to make
him all that he can become. Now you will at once
perceive that this very conception was impossible
until men had thought about *themselves.* Philosophy
in brief, though in a non-self-conscious form (I mean
not explicitly developed), was the necessary precursor
of the idea of education in its fulness; and philosophy was itself the product of religion, or one with it.
The relations of dependence and awe in which man
stood to the mysterious power by which he and all
his works were surrounded, and by which his best-
laid schemes were so often frustrated, led to thought
on this universal power and on man's relation to it.
Life and death and man himself became objects of
speculation; and as soon as men became capable of
the *thought of man,* they were competent to conceive
the thought of the growth of man to the full fruition
of his nature—in other words, the thought of his
education. But not sooner.

This thought—the thought of what man truly is
in his highest expression, which we may call the
*notion* of man, we owe, I have said, to the Greeks
more than to any other race.

# LECTURE II.

## THE END OF EDUCATION.

### PHILOSOPHY AS NECESSARY TO THE FORMATION OF A CONSCIOUS END OR IDEAL.

THE education of a human being then has at all times and in all circumstances a more or less conscious ideal in view. The ideal of successive races of mankind is the measure of their civilisation and their true history.

A conscious ideal is an ideal based on a study of man — in short, on the philosophy of man. But philosophy is not the subject of this Chair, and you must therefore be often content to rest satisfied with statements which cannot be presented to you in their full reasoned form, but rather wear a dogmatic aspect.

The ideal is also the end or purpose. The ideal end or purpose of education must manifestly be determined by the ideal end or purpose of human life itself.

To the question what this end or ideal in education may be, various answers have been given. All writers have found it necessary to propound some end or other, for they have felt the truth of what Jean Paul says, "The end desired must be known before the way. All means or art of education will be, in the

first instance, determined by the ideal or archetype
we entertain of it."

Montaigne's aim is summed up in the words, Wisdom and Virtue. Comenius gives as his aim, "Knowledge, Virtue, Religion." Milton's aim is Likeness to
God, best attained through Virtue and Faith. Locke's
aim is Health of Body, Virtue, and Good Manners.
The Pietists under Spener (died 1705) had for their
aim the building up of the Kingdom of God in the
heart of every child. Herbert Spencer's aim is stated
to be "Complete Living." A common German statement is, that the end is the harmonious development
of all the powers. I myself would prefer to say that
the ideal aim of education is the realisation of the
ideal of Man by each individual in and for himself.

All these answers, including my own, are so very
generalised as to be wholly uninstructive. Nor can
we find such instruction as to ends and ideals as shall
at the same time be a guide to us in educating, until,
among many universally admitted subordinate ends,
we can find that supreme end which governs all the
rest.

And to ascertain this we must first ascertain the
supreme and governing end of man's life.

This end is the Ethical Life.

The supreme end, then, of all education is an ethical end. The determination of this end and of the
conditions of its attainment constitutes the theory
and methodology of education.

The standard by which we ultimately judge a man
is his worth as a man — the outcome in life and con-

duct of all his capacities. " By their fruits ye shall know them; " and the fruit each yields is also the seed he sows. All special knowledges are of value only in so far as they contribute to the supreme ethical result. One man knows more Greek and Mathematics than another: is he *therefore* better educated? May it not be that just because one *knows* so very much more than another he is worse educated,— ethically a poor result? The actual outcome in bearing and conduct, which is life, is alone the test of our having fulfilled life.

Even in the technical education of a carpenter or weaver, I am fitting him to do his work better than he would otherwise do it — that is to say, more effectively, and therefore more honestly. I am qualifying him for industrial citizenship. The most efficient carpenter is, *qua* carpentering, the most moral carpenter. True, the most moral carpenter, in the larger sense, is not necessarily the most efficient carpenter: but he will desire to be the most efficient, because he has a moral ideal of manhood and of conduct as one citizen co-operating with other citizens for the industrial purposes of life. I give him technical instruction that he may be enabled to give effect in sound honest workmanship to his ideal of his own manhood and citizenship. Even technical instruction, then, has its moral purpose: it fits a man to be a true man in the social place he occupies. Thus, into everything we do, nay, into everything we think, the ethical element enters for better or worse.

But outside the question of man in his specific in-

dustrial and other relations to his fellow-men, there
is the question, of his manhood in its larger sense, his
fulfilment of himself simply as man; for we believe,
with the Athenians, that thereby we best fit him for
all his duties, whether of citizenship, or carpentering,
or anything else. How am I to ascertain wherein
man's fulfilment lies — his true life, that which governs all his relations?

Evidently only by inquiring into the nature of man
— his mental constitution, and his past history of
effort and failure. There, if anywhere, we shall find
what he is intended to be, and how he is intended to
act. But to do this we should have to deal with
Ethics in general, and this is not a Chair of Ethics,
but of Education. This much, however, we may say
bluntly — The education of a child is the bringing of
him up in such a way as to secure that when he is a
man he will fulfil his true life — not merely his life
as an industrial worker, not merely his life as a citizen, but his own personal life through his work and
through his citizenship.

But this is not all, for we have to consider the conditions of the attainment of the ethical end of education from the point of view, not only of the growth
of mind, but of the growth of body; for, "We have
not to train up a soul," says Montaigne, "nor yet a
body, but a man, and we cannot divide him." But
even the bodily conditions, important as they are, are
merely the basis of that which is higher.

First of all, I ask your attention to these physical
conditions.

# LECTURE III.

## BODY IN RELATION TO THE EDUCATION OF MIND.

MIND, we have said, is involved in matter or body — the "clay cottage," as Locke calls it. There can be no *mens sana* without *corpus sanum*. In discussing the question of the education of mind, it is assumed that healthy bodily conditions are first of all secured. Each day must be so arranged. as to provide the necessary time for physical exercise — especially in the form of play. Manual instruction in covered sheds, apart from its other uses, helps to maintain sound physical conditions, and in a climate like ours seems to be almost a necessity.

The physical or physiological conditions of mental receptivity and activity have also to be studied by the educator in their relation to healthy surroundings, to the amount of brain-work to be demanded from boys and girls, the length of school lessons, home lessons, and differences of power and of temperament.

*The following are the heads of a short course of Lectures on Physical Conditions:* —

(1) The Structure of the Human Body generally.

(2) The Blood and its Circulation — Waste — Nutrition — Purification.

(3) The Nerve-System — Sensory and Motor. The Senses. Muscular Activity.

(4) The Nerve-Apparatus of Receptivity and Activity; Gradual growth of this, and lessons to be drawn from the gradual growth.

(5) Waste of Nerve-Substance. Exhaustion of Nerve-Substance. Nutrition of Nerve-Substance.

(6) Memory and Habit as determined by physiological conditions.

(7) Reflex action : Automatic action : Secondarily-automatic action, and its educational significance.

*Summary of educational lessons to be drawn from a consideration of physical conditions: (a) Nutrition and Oxygenation of blood in brain (food and ventilation); (b) Rest; and variety of brain exercise; (c) Gradual growth of the intellectual and moral capacity in connection with growth of brain: the consequent limitation of the teacher's demands on pupils (length of lessons, etc.); (d) Habit of mind in so far as it is merely cerebral habit; (e) Gymnastic, with drill; (f) Sanitary conditions generally of intellectual and moral health and activity.*

*Books of Reference.* — Carpenter's *Mental Physiology;* M'Kendrick's *Elements of Physiology;* Professor Foster's *Primer.* These suffice for the student of education.[1]

---

[1] A complete course of physiology is not at all necessary for the student of education. A general knowledge of the human frame and of hygienic and cerebral conditions suffices. A course of four or five lectures illustrated by good diagrams will yield all the information needed.

Perhaps the most important lesson which physiology teaches in the domain of mind is that mind processes wear a kind of channel for themselves, so that, with practice, all mind activities, intellectual or moral, good or bad, flow more easily. Thus, things difficult to do become in the end so easy that the doing of them partakes of the character of automatic action. This kind of activity is called *secondarily-automatic.* On this point I would direct your attention to chap. iv. vol. i. of Professor James' *Principles of Psychology.*

Many important questions also are suggested by the relation of bodily growth to mental growth.

Under gymnastic, again, we have to compare the Greek gymnastic with British games, in respect of their recreative and moral influence as well as their power of promoting a balanced physical condition. Athleticism as opposed to a reasonable, or Greek, gymnastic must also receive consideration.

The recent movement in the direction of manual work is really an attempt to counterbalance the too exclusive demands which the school makes on intellect, and ought, in its due place, to be encouraged. The bearing of such work in its reflex effect on the intellect, as giving a certain firmness and solidity to purely intellectual operations, is also worthy of discussion. We must leave this whole subject for lecture-room treatment.

# LECTURE IV.

CONSCIOUSNESS, generally, is Mind.

The conscious subject is a one, self-identical mind-entity.[1] So far as mere consciousness is concerned, man and animals are like one another.

But man is more than a conscious animal, because he has reason, or *is* a reason. The fundamental form of reason makes its appearance with self-consciousness.

Man accordingly may be defined as a self-conscious rational mind-entity, involved in body.[2]

When the conscious or self-conscious entity has an object present to it, we call the former "subject," to distinguish it from the "object."

It appears then that the distinctive characteristic or difference of man as contrasted with other conscious beings, is Reason.

Accordingly, man being specifically a being of reason, the supreme end of human life, which has an inherent title to govern all other minor ends, must be the life of reason and in reason. Life is action, and, accordingly,

---

[1] This lecture is somewhat of the nature of a series of paragraphs to be fully expounded orally by the lecturer.

[2] *Vid.* Note A in the Appendix.

22

life in accordance with reason may be more fully expressed as a life of activity in the things of reason, and conduct in accordance with reason; and this, speaking generally, is what we have called the ethical life. Let us carry these propositions into more concrete detail.

*Moral and Spiritual Life.* — Life in the activity of reason, *i.e.* pure thought and contemplation, might with certain beings be the highest; but for man, since he can live at all only through multiform relations to the non-rational nature within him and to other things and persons, the issue of his life in conduct is the highest: that is to say, life in reason through his relations to things and persons, or, generally, life in relations as these are impregnated and moulded by reason. This is the *moral* life.

But man, by virtue of this same reason in him, has relations with the Infinite. Accordingly, when, in the life of thought and contemplation, man rises to the notion of God as Being and Thought-universal, and sees reason (which is also the truth) in relations, as in and through God, who is Reason-universal, — he then lives and acts in conscious communion with God as in all and through all. He now lives, not only the life of reason and in reason, but *with* Reason as the universal One in the many. This is the *spiritual* life.

But this spiritual life is only the moral life seen in God, and, so, the completion and fulness of the life of man.

The moral life, accordingly, when it has passed into the spiritual life, is what I mean by the Ethical Life.

*Note.* — In seeking the end or purpose of a complex organism like man, we have to fix on some thought and phrase which expresses at once the highest outcome and the *specific* functioning of his nature. He must, of course, first *be* what he *does;* but to stop at being, with a creature whose life consists in his relations to external things, circumstances, and, above all, to himself and other spirits like himself, would be to stop short of the completion of life, which does not consist in being and reverie, but in an activity determined by the state of being. We must, therefore, seek for some expression (if we are to have only one expression) which comprehends the essential activity of his nature, and denotes, at the same time, its purpose or end. The expression most comprehensive and least misleading is, I think, "ethical life."

Ethical life, then, is the spiritual life as including the *prior* moral life.

The moral life, as such, is rightly called the virtuous life. For this, there is manifestly necessary a virtuous state of being, and its sequel *effective virtue.* I may be full of virtuous sentiments and principles, but have very little effective virtue; I cannot, however, exhibit effective virtue save as the expression of a prior state of being.

Man, in so far as he is animal, has sensations and emotions like the animals. These give rise to desires, and impel him to do this or that. He differs from the animals by virtue of the reason in him, which regulates and directs these emotions and desires, and prescribes ends. The relations which these emotions and desires bear to each other, and to our fellow-men, are ascertained by reason interpreting experience;

and they get the name of "moral ideas," because they
are ideas determining action or conduct. These moral
ideas, *e.g.* justice, benevolence, integrity, courage,
truthfulness, purity, holiness, etc., constitute the
motives of a man's conduct, if he is moral. They
are sometimes called moral sentiments or virtues,
and the man who acts in accordance with them as *law*
of his nature, is said to be virtuous. The idea is at
once end and motive, but he can *fulfil* the idea only
through particular acts.

Man cannot act on these ideas until he possesses
them as knowledge (more or less distinct). If he
possesses these ideas and lives in the contemplation
of them, he may be said to be in a moral or virtuous
state of being; but his life is not fulfilled, nor is he
virtuous, till he gives effect to them in his daily conduct: till then, they are only half-born. This is
effective virtue — the virtuous or moral life. In education our main object is to train men to a habit of
effective virtue; but we desire also to elevate the
virtuous life, if we can, to the spiritual life, so that
the ethical life may be fulfilled in its wholeness in
each man.

*Note.* — There are many who keep their eyes so steadily
fixed on a man's acts, that they are disposed to look with
distrust on the inner growth of feeling and sentiment, or
what are commonly called moral ideas (and sometimes
"principles") — those inner motives which are a complex
of reason and emotion, and precede the possibility of virtue.
The giving effect to these in conduct is certainly, as effective
virtue, in advance of the mere state of mind which we call
"virtuous"; but as the cause must precede the effect, we

cannot afford in education to dispense with the consideration of the best way of creating the virtuous state of mind, simply as a contemplative state, with a view to the ultimate issue in action.

We shall find in practice, doubtless, that the wisest way of creating this virtuous *state*, is by getting the young (and ourselves) to act, *i.e.* to do the right and good thing, and in this way evoking the good emotion or sentiment. In other words, the generalised emotion or moral idea and the putting of it in practice, should, in training the young, be inseparably bound together as far as possible. By doing benevolent acts, for example, a child becomes a benevolent being, and entertains in consciousness and imagination — all ready for use — benevolent emotions.

At the same time, if we take the whole range of moral ideas, this way of procedure is impracticable, and we therefore try to build up in the child and youth a *system* of moral ideas which will constitute a permanent reservoir of motives always ready for use, whether in moral judgment or moral action.

Take the various moral ideas which constitute the motives of a good-will, viz. benevolence, justice, purity, honesty, integrity, truth-speaking, courage, resoluteness, perseverance, and so forth, and you will see how the growth of these in the mind (as furniture of the mind, so to speak) must be premised if we are to secure our result — effective virtue — in all conditions and circumstances.

If we cannot create these generalised feelings or ideas, and give them lodgment in the minds of the young by regulating all their petty acts, how are we to supplement our want of opportunity? We shall get a full answer to this in the sequel; but meanwhile I would say *generally*, that we supplement the ordinary experiences of life in three ways:— 1. By authority and precept. 2. By our own example. 3. By getting children to contemplate the acts of others, either as they see them going on before their eyes, or, through imagination, by the help of narratives and poetry. (But this is to anticipate the discussion on method.)

The moral life and the spiritual life (in brief, the ethical life) must exist as a system of ideas and motives before it is active, and consequently presumes for its existence an antecedent activity of reason in ascertaining, or accepting, ethical ideas and ends. Hence the importance in education of so training the intelligence of all that each, though incapable of ascertaining for himself the ideas which nourish the moral and spiritual nature, may yet acquiesce in them with intelligence and personal conviction, make them his own, and not be merely the slave of dogma, misapprehended or not apprehended at all. Man is an ethical being only so far as he is a *self*-regulated being.

Men have, happily, not to depend each on the activity of his own reason for the ascertainment of the truth of life and conduct — the moral ideas which are to constitute his ever-present motives. They inherit the fruit of the labours of past generations. As regards its substance generally, indeed, education is Tradition — the handing on of intellectual and moral possessions by those set apart as competent for the task.

We may now conclude that the supreme end of education is the ethical life, and that the main instrument in training to the *substance* of this is tradition;[1] and that reason in each has to be so trained that the young may intelligently acquiesce, and so make the transmitted moral and spiritual life *their own.*

---

[1] "There is a history in all men's minds
Figuring the nature of the times deceased." — 2 *Henry IV.* iii.

The transmitters of this tradition are primarily the parent and schoolmaster.

But, further, the ethical life is not only the Good, but the LAW for man, *because* it comprehends the ideas of his relations to things and persons — the *truth* for life and conduct. By the fulfilment of this law alone, can a man fulfil or realise himself; and, accordingly, he owes *duty* to the law.

The reason of man is by its very nature always seeking for law, and we consequently meet its necessities by bringing him under a sense of the law which is inherent in the truth of his relations; and we accustom him, when young, to obey the law though he cannot yet see the truth of it for himself. Thus we strengthen the connate perception of law in him, and habituate him to act in accordance with certain ideas or truths as law, and because of the duty he owes to law.

When a youth perceives the truth of the moral ideas which ought to determine conduct, and has acquired a habit of duty to them, he is educated morally. The spiritual education may accompany or follow this; and then there is realised the full ethical life in him, *i.e.* activity of reason or intelligence whereby he perceives the truth and obeys the law, and leads the life of law in God. The ethical life in a man then (to sum up) is a habit of action in accordance with moral ideas as the divine order, under a sense of duty to the law inherent in them as spiritual or divine law.

This may seem all very general; but, in very truth,

the significance of all we teach and of every lesson we give is ethical — always ethical, or it is, in its educational reference, wholly insignificant or rather non-significant. True, we have to educate experts in the various departments of human activity in order that the torch of learning and of civilisation may be held high and handed on. But the education of a nation does not aim at this, but at something much greater. A school accordingly is not to be judged as an educational institution by the number of its "scholars," but by its ethical results, including, as the precondition of such results, bodily vigour.

Our constant aim in studying the science of education must be to bring all philosophic discussions and conclusions to a practical issue. We have to deduce rules for our guidance.

The supreme end is always, it is presumed, with us, and is daily and hourly influencing us in what we teach or deliberately omit to teach ; but, besides exercising this governing function, it yields a principle of method which helps us in our teaching. For the end contemplated is a practical end ; it is the issue of intellect and of moral and spiritual ideas in a habit of action ; it is a *turning to use* — the use of life, of all the furniture and trained activity of mind.

*Principle of Method.* — TURN TO USE.

Accordingly, this principle should be constantly applied in every subject we teach and in every lesson in every subject. We see the rule illustrated by a

good teacher of mathematics, who knows that his business is not to make mathematical experts, but to use
mathematics in so far as it contributes to the general
education of the human mind. Every theorem understood has its consequences. The practical relations of
geometry to mensuration and geometrical drawing,
and the deduction of riders to be worked out independently by the pupils, are never omitted from his
course. He is indifferent to the amount of Euclid
"gone over"; his business is to pause and to make
sure by means of deductions that the intellectual discipline and the practical application are insured. In
brief, at every stage he "turns to use."

So with the good teacher of language: he turns
everything to use from the first lesson onwards.

The ultimate and sole effective test of all knowledge
in every department is — Can the pupil *use* it?

# LECTURE V.

THE spiritual life is not achieved except through the habit of virtuous activity, and in like manner the virtuous life is not fulfilled until it passes into the spiritual life. The ethical life, accordingly, is not a state of *being* solely, but a continued series of ethical *acts* bound together by an ideal of life. If this be so, and if the ethical life be the supreme end of education, the analysis of the elements (moments or steps) of an ethical act ought to yield to us the *Educative Process* generally.

I find that the ethical act, as a final willing of the good, contains the following elements : —

1. Right judgment as to the facts before us and their relations: a process of reason. (Substance of knowledge and power of discrimination.)

2. A moral idea (at the heart of which there is always an emotion) following on the clear perception of the facts; which idea incites or attracts us to act in accordance with itself: and this we call our motive of action (at once end and motive). (Substance of morality.)

3. Willing or action in accordance with the said motive-idea under a sense of duty to it as Law — a

31

sense of imperative obligation (itself by itself also a motive).  (Moral discipline.)

4. The perception of the idea as in God and of the law as Divine.  (Religion.)

If I *will* in accordance with the idea (taking it into myself, and making it part of my character for the occasion), I have a resultant sense of harmony, non-contradiction, or peace, which is always the inner guarantee of the attainment of ethical completeness.

*Note* 1. — Let me repeat that when I say that the end of the education of the young is effective virtue resting on a virtuous state of being, in other words, the habit of virtue, I do not use these words in a vague sense.  The virtuous life is not a life of contemplation, but of action; it is not an abstract, but a concrete made up of a series of daily and hourly virtuous acts.  We do not wish to rear citizens who talk about the virtuous life, and walk about displaying moral placards, but citizens who quietly do their duty as a matter of course, and are ever watchful over themselves in all the details of business and of social and family intercourse.  A large part of the virtuous life must always consist in the efficient doing of the work for which we get wages, whether that work be carrying bricks or guiding the State.  To be always virtuous is so difficult that there is no energy left for ostentatiously talking about it.

*Note* 2. — The educator must always keep chiefly in view the primary demands that may be legitimately made on all men — a virtuous state of being and effective virtue.  The spiritual, which is the essence of all religion, will accompany or follow.  When we have trained to the ethical life in its completeness we have built the temple.  The activity of reason in things of reason, the enjoyment of the beautiful in nature and art, and the graces and courtesies of manner and intercourse (εὐκοσμία), all go, doubtless, to the ideal fulfilment of a man.  But our business is with the temple, before we concern ourselves with its decoration. The rational and the æsthetic for their own sake will always receive the attention of the educator, especially in their ethical relations; but we cannot afford to think of them save as accessory to the ethical life.

The Educational *End*, as I conceive it, might now be stated thus : —

RIGHT JUDGMENT AND A HABIT OF GOOD ACTION UNDER A SENSE OF DUTY, ACCOMPANIED BY A COMPREHENSION OF THE SPIRITUAL SIGNIFICANCE OF NATURE AND MAN.

The Educative *Process*, as that is revealed by the analysis of the ethical act, is, speaking generally, a process of Instruction and of Discipline.

A. — *Instruction* (*Knowledge*).

(1) Instruction in our relations to things and persons, commonly called intellectual instruction.

(2) Instruction in moral ideas, commonly called moral instruction (the virtues). (The Good.)

(3) Instruction in the spiritual, *i.e.* the religious idea. (God.)

B. — *Training and Discipline* (*Faculty*).

(1) Training and discipline to the habit of *intelligent* or *rational* activity.

(2) Training and discipline to the habit of virtuous willing, *i.e.* good action under a sense of duty.

(3) Training to the spiritual habit of mind.

The educative process, as so conceived, gives us a systematic view of the whole field of education, outside the presupposed physical conditions.

## A. — INSTRUCTION.

### *The Realistic and the Humanistic.*

To give the materials of right judgment we have to instruct the young. It has been usual to oppose to one another real (realistic) instruction and humanistic — the former being instruction in those things that concern a man's *nature*-environment; the latter, instruction in the relations of men to each other, and in the creations of man as a being of reason, *i.e.* literature, art, and all thought on that which is specifically human. The humanistic has also been identified with Greek and Latin literature, because at the time of the Renaissance the best literature was to be found in those languages. A little thought suffices to show that there is hopeless confusion in such distinctions. Literature and the things of thought are in a much truer sense realities than the things of sense, and all literature and art, ancient or modern, is equally humanistic. The best division of subjects is into the Real and the Formal or Abstract, corresponding to the two demands of instruction and discipline; and

these again have each to be divided into Naturalistic
and Humanistic; thus:

I. — *The Real (with a view chiefly to Nutrition of Mind).*

(a) *The Real-Naturalistic:*

(1) Knowledge of the world of nature by which the
pupil is surrounded. (In its initial stages
this includes lessons in colour, form, measure,
weight, number, sound, and object-lessons
generally: in later stages, a knowledge of
animals, plants, and manufactured products.)

(2) Knowledge of that part of nature nearest to
the pupil himself, viz. his own body, with
special relation to the laws of health.

(3) The distribution of men and nations, with the
physical conditions of their lives and their
related industrial and commercial characteristics. This, with topography, constitutes
school geography.

(4) Physiography.

(b) *The Real-Humanistic:*

(1) Language, *i.e.*
(a) The vernacular language as the expression
of the thought of others. Literature.
(b) The vernacular language as the expression
of one's own thought, a synthetic exercise. (Imitative composition, with a
view to the correct use of language.)

(2) Foreign languages *as literature*.

(3) Economics.
(4) History, with civil relations.
(5) Moral instruction [including minor morals].
(6) Spiritual ideas, including religious truth.

### Subsidiary Subjects:

Art.
   (*a*) Music.
   (*b*) Appreciation of the arts of painting, sculpture, and architecture.

## B. — TRAINING AND DISCIPLINE.

II. — *The Formal or Abstract (with a view chiefly to Discipline of Mind).*

| (*a*) *Naturalistic.* | (*b*) *Humanistic.* |
|---|---|
| Drawing. | Grammar. |
| Arithmetic. | Rhetoric.[1] |
| Mathematics. | Logic.[1] |

The formal or abstract chiefly *discipline* the mind and give power; the real *feed* the mind and give nutrition.

To give adequate instruction in all these studies to all is impossible; but the instruction of all should be on these lines, carried as far as time permits, and given in such a way as will lead to the further voluntary prosecution of them.

---

[1] Rhetoric and Logic are not to be formally taught till the pupil has reached the university stage.

Reading and writing, as instruments whereby we receive the thoughts of others and convey our own, are, of course, primary elements in all education; but, were it not that they are necessary as instruments for bringing the mind into contact with the naturalistic, humanistic, and the formal in knowledge, we should not think of wasting time over them.

The above are our materials of *instruction* — the food we give; and they are also the subjects by which we discipline and train the intelligence and moral nature of the young to an ethical result. There are, within the range of school life, up to the end of the secondary period (the eighteenth year), no other subjects having equal claims.

*Liberal and Technical Education.* — All the above studies enter into a "liberal" education. Here again we have to define. A liberal education is the education of a man for the sake of his manhood, and up to an ideal of manhood, without regard to any *specific* use to which he may turn his knowledge and powers. Doubtless, there is a sense in which all education is for use — the uses of life and living; but by the "useful" is usually understood the materially useful, that which enables a man to *earn his living.* Hence the term to be opposed to "liberal" in education is "technical," that is to say, instruction and training with reference to certain industrial uses and material results. "Professional" education is thus so far technical, and is to be distinguished from industrial technical education only in so far as it rests on more advanced, and on liberal, studies.

All thinkers on education of any importance con-
tend for a liberal education — the education of the
man; believing that thereby they best fit all men for
the work of the world generally, no less than for the
specific function each has to discharge as a member
of a co-operative community.

Whatever we teach for its own sake, with a view
to the ideal of man solely, is an element of liberal
education. Even manual instruction, not to speak of
the elements of science, falls under this designation.
All depends on the purpose we have in view, whether
it be general or special.

The Athenians held that the best men — simply as
men — made the best citizens; the Spartans, though
Hellenic in their general conceptions of education,
had a more restricted view. Their ideal of man was
the soldier, and their training was, in truth, technical
in the gymnastic and military sense; and, so far, it
was a debased Greek form.

Culture is a vague term; but when we speak of a
" man of culture," we certainly mean a man of liberal
education. And if our definition of a liberal education be correct, a man may be a man of culture though
destitute of Latin and Greek. On the other hand, inasmuch as a liberal education has regard to the ideal
of " man," it follows (and is a fact admitted by all)
that the humanistic or *man*-subjects promote a liberal
education, and consequent culture, in a sense which
realistic studies do not. A man trained solely on the
latter cannot be liberally educated; a man trained
solely on the former can, on the contrary, be liberally

educated. In short, what is called "culture" is not within reach of the man trained solely on the real-naturalistic, but it is attainable by the man trained solely on the real-humanistic. At the same time, naturalistic subjects, I admit, might be so taught as to be humanised, and thus come within the sphere of the humanistic.

# LECTURE VI.

## MATERIALS IN THEIR RELATION TO THE NUTRITION OF MIND.

WE have now to consider the real elements of education, naturalistic and humanistic, one after the other, and ascertain what is the precise significance of each for man, and in what sense they contribute to his nutrition. Always limiting our range of view to the termination of what is called the period of "secondary" instruction, — the age of seventeen complete, — we have to ascertain how much of each subject ought to be acquired within that period with a view to the regulation of life — right judgment and good action.

Two governing considerations must accompany us in this inquiry, and be assumed throughout.

1. Whatever subjects we teach, each should be *so* taught from the beginning, that at whatever age social necessities may interrupt the course of instruction, the pupil shall have received all the benefit from it which his age admits of.

2. Inasmuch as the supreme end is always ethical, instruction in every subject, and at every stage of that subject, should be dominated by this end as regards its quantity, quality, and method.

**40**

[Here follows a consideration of real subjects in detail and their educational values, — considered as materials or substance of knowledge. The discussion extends over five or six lectures, which would too much encumber this book.]

*Note.* — Though it is to anticipate, let me here say a word as to the *Instruction-Plan.* There has been much writing on the question of the organisation of schools — primary, secondary, and so forth. The organisation of a school is an external matter, and sums itself up in the time-table.

A far more important question is the *organisation of the instruction;* and the first difficulty here is the selection of subjects which we think boys and girls ought to have studied by the time they reach the age of seventeen complete, and *how much* of each.

Then, we have to determine the amount and nature of the instruction in each subject at the different stages of mental growth. Every age has its own studies. The knowledge of each and every subject taught must grow with the growth of the mind we are educating, and not anticipate it. If it anticipate it, the result of the instruction is not knowledge, but rote-information.

The organisation of instruction is a difficult task. It is not at all necessary for educational purposes that boys and girls of seventeen should know much of anything, but *it is essential that they know thoroughly, according to a sound method, what they profess to know,* and that, when they leave school, they find themselves, through the skill and devotedness of their teachers, in a rational attitude to all knowledge.[1] I shall illustrate the quantity of knowledge to be conveyed, and its gradation, when I speak in detail of applied method. The amount, however, is of little value compared with the

---

[1] I am well aware that with some boys and girls such results are unattainable; none the less do they constitute the teacher's aim and ideal.

result in respect of intellectual exactness, intellectual interest, and intellectual power.

———

We have now before us the Ethical End in its full statement. We have also laid down the Educative Process in general; and dealt with the first part of the process, viz. Right Judgment, in so far as this is dependent on mere knowledge. We have further surveyed the materials of this knowledge — the subjects which a youth of seventeen ought to have studied, distinguishing those which are essential and those which, though only accessory, are yet important. However much more a youth may know, these things (pp. 34, 35, 36) he ought to know, if he is to be fitly educated for the work of life and his ethical function in life. The youth of active mind will extend his knowledge far beyond any limits which we might think it reasonable to set; but all extension beyond these limits has to do with the elevation of the plane of intellectual and ethical life and the reach of the mental horizon, rather than with that knowledge which is imperative for all.

# LECTURE VII.

To Right Judgment is necessary, not only knowledge, but an active, vigorous, and discriminating intelligence. The saying, "Knowledge is power," is only a half-truth; for, without an active and vigorous intellect, it may be a burden and an obstruction. When we consider that the mere experience of life, apart from books and schools, may give man almost all he wants for the moral guidance of his life in all ordinary matters, if only he can bring to bear on that experience a perspicacious, penetrating, and interpreting intellect, we feel that power alone is power, and that knowledge — the accumulated results of experience — must take a second place in the education of a human being. At the same time, it is scarcely correct to say that training and discipline are of more importance than knowledge. Mathematics, for example, disciplines the intelligence; and we can easily conceive a mind admirably disciplined by mathematics, but conspicuously faulty in judgment because of its ignorance of the real and concrete relations of things into which moral and æsthetic elements *always* largely enter. So with all pure discipline as such. Accord-

43

ingly, the substance of knowledge acquired — the food
or nutrition of mind, is of more importance than some
educationalists are disposed to think. Let us say
that instruction and discipline are, in fact, of equal
moment. Instruction, however, naturally first engages
our attention when we have a mind to educate. There
is a void before us which we have to fill.

Now we can *instruct*, in a sense, without giving any
appreciable training and discipline to the intelligence.
For our instruction may be merely information — facts
which the pupil commits to memory ; the reducing of
these to rational cohesion being left to the chapter
of accidents. The acquiring of information, simply as
information and as an exercise of memory, is what is
meant by rote-instruction. Among other evils attend-
ing such a mode of conveying knowledge is this, that
it cannot possibly interest and attract the intellect, or
the moral and spiritual nature, of a human being; and
thus, a distaste for learning and a silent antagonism
to the teacher, and also to authority generally, are
generated. Accordingly, it has been found necessary
to inflict physical chastisement, and to appeal to fear
in various other forms, in order to compel the majority
of boys to do the work of rote-acquisition. In truth,
this way of instructing is always necessarily accompanied with severity of discipline; and hence, the
teacher or magister has been popularly known through
all the ages as pedant, dominie, castigator puerorum,
plagosus, and so forth.

Again, we may instruct intelligently, but with a
view to discipline alone. In that case, we equally fail

to interest the young mind, and so to achieve our ultimate intellectual purpose, which is the placing of the
mind in an attitude of rational activity to all knowledge. Such an attitude can exist only when there is
interest as well as discipline. The growing body cannot be fed by a series of difficult exercises in digest-
ing, but only by food which it can readily assimilate
and digest. So with the mind: it demands feeding,
and the food must be of a kind that it can digest and
assimilate if it is to grow either in knowledge or in
power, and above all, in intellectual interest.

These considerations place us, as students of the
science and art of education, in a critical position.
Are the questions of assimilation of knowledge and
of discipline to power different questions which yield
us answers involving mutual contradiction ? If so,
our case as educationalists would be a bad one; for
we should have to follow two different methods in
order to attain the two different ends — nutrition and
discipline. Fortunately it is not so ; the best method
of instructing with a view to assimilation, is also the
best method of training and disciplining with a view
to power, as we shall see. The educational problem
is thus simplified.

In the preceding paragraph I have assumed that
there is such a thing as Method : and a method may
be good, better, or best. Indeed, the etymology of the
word "instruction" would of itself suggest to us that
there is method, for it implies the building of one

course on another in a certain order with a view to the completing of a structure.

All will admit that there must be *some* method of instructing: and further, that the best method must be that which follows the way in which the fabric of mind builds itself up. This, indeed, is the ultimate form in which the question of educational method must be put. This is also, let it be noted, *the* ultimate question of all psychology (and to a large extent of metaphysics also), so closely are the philosophy of mind and the education of mind connected. The answer to the one question is the answer to the other. But the student of education asks the question always with a practical purpose, and especially with distinct reference to the building up or *growing* of mind. He does not, in a mere abstract interest, analyse the complex result before him — the adult mind ; but mind in its process of gradual formation: and even this abstract question he investigates with a view to a further question, viz. " What can I wisely do to help mind to grow so that it may reach a certain ideal standard of knowledge and power? " All the traditionary words that have to do with the bringing up of the young point etymologically to this, as that which underlies all the particular problems of the family and the school, *e.g.* "education," "training," "instruction," "discipline."

The best method of instruction, I have said, is also happily, the best method of disciplining. We may fix our attention, then, on the method of instructing, since we shall find that the method of discipline is therein also contained. By a sound method of instruction we shall find that we best train and discipline the mind, and by a sound method of training and discipline we shall find that we best instruct it. This will appear more clearly as we go along. In the meantime, as we have already defined the term "instruct," let us now endeavour, before going further, to find whether there is any distinction between "training" and "disciplining" — two words which I have generally used together, as if in their combination they expressed one notion.

"Training" and "disciplining" are essentially the same process; but there is a distinction.

To train the intelligence, is to carry it, or lead it, through the various steps which end in the knowledge of anything, *e.g.* I lead a boy, step by step, through the processes which end in his adequate comprehension of the demonstration of a geometrical theorem, and I thus *train* his intelligence, inasmuch as I guide him through intelligent processes; and in so far as I *accustom him* to such processes. He reconstructs in his own mind, by my help and imitatively, the thought of the original mathematician, and the thinking process in him is thereby trained. Now, to discipline is the same as to train, with this difference, that I call on the boy to initiate *for himself,* and carry through for himself without my help, the processes which end in the demonstration of a theorem or problem ; as, for example, when I set a rider. To do this a boy has to think more closely, to apply *himself* more intensely,

and in finding out the steps of proof for himself
he *approaches* more closely thought in itself, — the
processes of reason as such, and the conditions of its
satisfaction.

Discipline of intelligence, accordingly, is the self-
initiated activity of intelligence with a view to an end.
Approximately, it is the abstract exercise of intelligence. Thus it is that formal or abstract studies
discipline much more surely and effectively than
real studies do : they demand self-sustained and self-
directed application.

Every mental act which involves self-conscious unaided effort is of the nature of discipline.

Training and discipline are thus constantly, in practice, passing into each other.

Let it now be admitted that if a master, when instructing in a subject, does so *in such a way* as to train
and discipline the intelligence by means of the subject,
he will thereby not only best accomplish this important part of his educational task, but, at the same
time, best give instruction. A "war" is a "method,"
and we are now brought face to face with METHO-
DOLOGY — i.e. *the way of best instructing, that so we may
best train and discipline, the intelligence.*

[I postpone the question of the Training and Discipline of the moral and spiritual nature.]

# LECTURE VIII.

## METHODOLOGY AND ITS SCIENTIFIC BASIS.

IT now appears that we best *instruct* if we pursue the method of instruction which best trains and disciplines, and that we best *train* and *discipline* if we pursue the best method of instruction.

Now, the way or method of instruction is, in brief, the way or method of *knowing*, or learning. To teach with perfect success, the teacher must put himself in the position and attitude of the pupil who, being ignorant, desires to know.

It is beyond all question that we can say nothing rationally of the method of knowing without analysing the process whereby mind as a matter of fact knows; that is to say, appropriates and makes use of the raw materials presented to it with a view to the building up of the fabric of knowledge. Doubtless we might collect together the *results* of such an analysis, as propounded by some well-known writer on philosophy, and give them to you as a dogmatic system, under the name of "Rules of Procedure, or Methods." We might then apply these rules, one by one, under the head of "Applied Method," to instruction in this, that, or the other subject, and show how they worked out. And this would itself be a great gain. But it would not be the *Science* of method, or the scientific study of method, but only the more or less slavish acquisition of the rules of the art of instructing and disciplining the intelligence. These rules, when further extended to moral and religious instruction and training, would constitute the whole art of education — an art based on science, it is true, but not studied as a science by you, the teacher, and, therefore, dead, as mere dogma always must be.

Accordingly, if we are to proceed scientifically and introduce the teacher to the science or philosophy of his art, enable him to see the principles which guarantee and inspire method, and how it is that they contribute effectually to our supreme ethical end, we must ask him to analyse with us the process of knowing: in other words, we must ask him to study the psychology of intelligence from the point of view of the *growth* of intelligence. While dwelling for a time in this abstract region, we shall always keep steadily in view our practical aim. It is not psychology as an abstract study that here concerns us, but psychology in its relations to the education of mind, that is to say, psychology in so far as it yields the Art of education as a system of principles; or, briefly, as Methodology.

I have now, accordingly, to ask you to accompany me into the abstract field of the philosophy of mind with special reference to education. Apart from its professional importance to you, it must be accepted as part of your academic discipline. For I hold that the study of education is itself an education, and rightly claims a position among university disciplines; and that not in the interests of school-teaching alone: for the philosophy of education is a philosophy of life.

*Note.*— It will be said that all of us, whether boys or men, learn something somehow, whatever the method of teaching, and that very clever boys learn a great deal. If scientific method is of so much importance, how is this to be accounted for? In answer to this question I would submit the following considerations :—

1. As a matter of fact, the great majority of boys learn very little, and get no mental discipline worth mentioning.

2. The proportion of those who learn anything is greater in primary schools than in secondary, and this simply because primary teachers are as a rule alive to method (such as it is).

3. All boys learn something, it is said, and some boys learn a good deal spite of bad teaching. True, and the explanation of this is that human reason is a pure activity, and that it either shirks a difficulty and turns to something else, or it seeks *of itself* to reduce to order and method the confused lessons of the master. The abler minds accomplish this task : the great majority cannot do so, and never do so.

4. It is universally admitted that boys learn more, and get better discipline, from a good teacher than from a bad one, and that many good, and some admirable, teachers have been untrained. But if we look closely we shall find that the "good" teacher is a man who *instinctively* follows good methods, whether he knows it or not. The philosophy or theory of education includes the questions of end, of the educative process, of the materials of instruction and of method. Now, the earnest teacher has always in his mind *some* theory more or less vague; and having end, general process, and materials clearly present to him, he instinctively, if he is as able as he is earnest, finds, ere long, a way or

method of instruction which is fairly good. Also, because
he is earnest in his work, he relies largely on moral stimulus.
This is the sort of man we call a "good" teacher, and
whose success we admire. The object of the study of education as a science and an art is simply to bring the end,
process, and materials *early* into clear consciousness in the
case of this naturally good teacher, and to show him, before
he begins, the best way or method of doing his daily work,
and so making it even more effective than it is. As regards
all other teachers (the vast majority), the object is to raise
them to the level of the "good" teacher — a level which they
could never attain but by the help of instruction in their
professional work. The study of education, in short, makes
the good master better and brings the inferior master up to
a fair average, and in very many cases, indeed, makes him a
thoroughly good teacher, as the results of our primary training colleges have amply proved.

· Then, quite apart from this practical aim, the study of
education places the whole profession on a higher intellectual
plane. Whatever raises the schoolmaster's conception of
his task makes him a better man. Whatever instructs him
as to his duties, makes him a better teacher. A firm hold,
moreover, of end, principles, and method gives him faith in
his daily work.

# SECOND PART.

## THE PHILOSOPHY OF INTELLIGENCE AS YIELDING THE METHODOLOGY OF EDUCATION.

# LECTURE I.

## THE ANIMAL MIND.

POET and peasant are alike in this, that they are dependent on tradition. Differ as they may in temperament and in the quality of nerve-tissue, their minds would at the beginning of their life-career be blank, were it not for the inheritance which parents and society pass on to them. The form and outer expression of a man's poetic possibilities are as dependent on the imagery of feeling and of thought, and on the store of language to which he succeeds, as on the materials of his present environment. The peasant, again, finds his standard of life, and a way of judging things and of using the instruments of a struggle with nature, ready-made for him. Tradition is the handing on of the achievements of the past, and all are alike dependent on it. The schoolmaster plays an important part as one of the chief vehicles of transmission. Whether aptitudes, moral and intellectual, acquired during each generation's life are also handed on, has lately been doubted by the biologist. If it be really so, the progress of humanity is less assured than it was thought to be ten or twenty years ago. The power of the existing generation in influencing the future of our race is lessened; but the teacher's responsibilities as the transmitter of the past are not thereby diminished, but rather increased.

With animals there is no tradition of recorded victories; and if the new theory be accepted, no tradition even of acquired aptitudes. They simply inherit a certain constitution, and they have to make the best of it in an ever-renewed contest with nature. They have mind as we have; but mind within certain restrictions of faculty.

If we are to understand the human mind, we cannot do better than try to understand and to interpret the animal mind in its highest forms, for we shall thereby ascertain in what respects we differ from animals. We, too, are animals; but something more. It is because we, as self-conscious subjects, are animal and something more, that we are able, by observing the lower organisms around us, to say something regarding them, and get some light on what man is and can be. If we take the human mind by itself, without regard to other and lower stages of mind, we are apt to commingle elements which ought to be kept distinct, and to interpret phenomena in a confused and often self-contradictory way.

We certainly share with the higher class of animals, not only the feeling of life-activity and life-impulse generally, but specific forms of these. All our appetites, as determined by our bodily needs, the outgoing feelings and desires which enter into our scheme of moral motives — *e.g.* the feeling of goodwill or kindness to others, a feeling of the supremacy of

certain things over us (in animals little more than
fear, which suggests escape from the presence of that
which is felt to be more powerful), and a feeling of
satisfaction or complacence in the goodwill or kindness of others towards us.

Let me illustrate. When a lion and lioness are
lying with their cubs in a cavern, the lioness licking
her young or giving to them of the fruit of her own
body, or such fragments of the chase as she may have
brought home from her last raid, while the attendant
lion growls defiantly on hearing a crackling among
the reeds which he associates with a wild elephant
or boa-constrictor, we have all the primitive feelings
which I have above summarised in one tableau. In
addition, we have the feeling of resistance to an external power as threatening the life of the family. Nay,
more, we must at once see that the community of
tenderness rests on a primary *bond* between the members of this group, which is Sympathy — that is, the
feeling of the feelings of others, and the consequent
presence of a disposition to satisfy the feelings and
desires of others, in so far as these betoken a need of
any kind.

This is a picture, not only of the animal, but of the
primitive man in his primitive relations, which he
can no more help than he can help eating when he is
hungry or drinking when he is thirsty.

But at this point the lion stops; whereas the man,
his wife, and children in the stone cave have in them
possibilities, which may be said to be (speaking
loosely) infinite, though always restricted by racial
characteristics and possibilities.

Let me point out, that in addition to the bodily
appetites which have to do with self-preservation,
propagation, etc., we have in the above lion-group
sympathy, kindness towards others, a pleasing sensation in receiving kindness from others, a feeling of an
actual or possible higher power, and of resistance to
that power as threatening the life or happiness of
the lion and his family.  We can easily imagine the
approach of a force so great as to overpower resistance by anticipation, and cause fear for life and a
rapid retreat for safety.

What now have we here as instincts ?

1. Bodily appetites concerned in the preservation
of life and the continuity of the species.

2. Sympathy.

3. Goodwill to others.

4. Love of the goodwill of others.

5. Feeling of superior power and dependence on it.

6. Fear.

7. Resistance to drive off danger to life (animal
courage).

If man were no more than this bundle of needs, in
the form of appetitive impulses and desires, which we
find in the lion, he would not be man; he would not
be even the king of beasts (save in the range of his
sympathy, of which more hereafter), for the lion
would soon make short work of him.  So much for
the feelings and impulses, which we call instincts,
because they are connate.  Let us consider, next, the
phenomena which we call the intelligence of the
animal.

We have to go beyond mere feelings and impulses, and their inevitable manifestation in certain circumstances, as, *e.g.* when the lion roars defiance in the circumstances we have supposed, viz. the approach of an alarming power. This necessity of going beyond mere feeling is forced upon us, if by nothing else than by this, that the feelings of which we have been speaking arise only after something else has happened in the economy of the lion-mind.

*That* something else is seeing, hearing, and tactile-sensation. Make your lion deaf, and blind, and insensible to touch, and nothing happens as we have described it.

Certain impressions are made on what we call his consciousness, because he becomes conscious or *aware* of them, through his eyes, his ears, and his skin. He feels these impressions in his conscious living subject — the impression of a crackling in the reeds, of the sudden presentation of a wild elephant or boa-constrictor, and of the personal contact of his lioness and her whelps. These impressions are impressions of noise, touch, size, shape, motion, colour (in this rudimentary sense at least, that the colour of the elephant is different from the impression made by the surrounding atmosphere and the forest).

The ear and the tactual sensibility thus furnish materials or facts to the lion's consciousness as they do to ours, but not to the same extent, or with the same delicacy or variety as the eyes do, for they are the chief channels of communication with the outer world. We shall, therefore, drop here all reference (except as it may arise incidentally) to any channel of sense-impression save the eyes. This we do in view of the task before us, and because what is true of the eyes is true, *mutatis mutandis,* of other organs of communication between the mind or consciousness of the lion and the external world in which he lives, and with which he has the hard work of correlating himself, in the interests of himself and his family, so as to secure a pleasing or instinct-satisfied existence.

I would at this point emphasise the phenomenon of Feeling in presence of a presentation as the most universal and primary experience of animal being. It is the starting-point of all manifestations of consciousness, and lies at the root of all that animal and man are and can be.

Feeling cannot in any strict logical sense be defined; but it can be marked off from other experiences, and in contrast with them. It is a vague and indefinite awareness of a movement within the subject effected by a stimulus within, or from without, the physical organism. Without feeling there could be no beginning of conscious life, and in the highest expressions of even self-conscious reason it is the ultimate guarantee that there is anything present at all. In the most abstract mathematical process a man in the energy of pursuit is not self-conscious of that process, and cannot be so until he makes that process an object to himself; but, all the while, he is supported by the vague and indefinite feeling of conscious activity — a *feeling* and nothing more.

When an animal or an infant-man (passing over
the preliminary experiences of life) opens his eyes,
his nerve system, and through this his consciousness,
becomes aware, through the external stimulus which
we call an impression, of an universal extensity in
which nothing is defined, all is confused and chaotic.
Subject and object are, though not identical in fact,
yet identical in feeling. There is no separation of
feeling-subject from felt-object, still less is there
separation of one object from another. We know
that there must be a reaction in the nerve-cells, but it
is not sufficiently energetic to reflect the stimulus as
something *not* the subject feeling.

By dint of continuous and oft-repeated impact the
reaction becomes gradually more energetic, and the
external stimulus B is placed outside as *not* the feel-
ing-consciousness A.

Generally it will be found that in its earliest manifestations this feeling of a not-A is restricted to a
single point, and does not embrace the totality of the
stimulating or impressing B. For example, a snail,
instinctively putting out its organ of sensation, touches
a rough stone and turns aside, or a leaf and takes possession of it; it does not feel the stone or leaf in their
respective totalities as stone or leaf, but feels only a
certain repulsion or attraction limited to a single
point. So, in the vegetable unconscious world we
have an anticipation of this conscious action, as in the
fly-catcher. There is more than vague feeling so far
as the snail is concerned; there is a definite feeling
of a "single" which is not-A; and I would call this

punctual consciousness "sensation" in its lowest form, and assign to it the name *Sensibility.*

It would require a patient, critical, and sympathetic observation of the infant and animal mind to say at what point a stimulating object is more than this unit of sensation which I have called sensibility. To determine the passage of one stage of consciousness from a lower to a higher is probably impossible, because all things progress by infinitely small steps. None the less is the step taken, as we see from the result. At what fraction of a moment the hour-hand on a dial-plate points to twelve, I cannot tell, but at one moment it had not arrived and at another it had passed it.

The next stage of consciousness of a definite kind worthy of notice here, is the *feeling* of total objects *as totals.* But it is manifestly impossible to feel a total save in so far as other totals emerge from the chaotic confusion of the extended manifold and are *felt* as there, and yet as not the particular total B, which for the moment specifically impresses, attracts, and occupies consciousness.

The feeling of a total as not-A (A being the subject) but B, is the feeling of B as an object. There is here a distinctly emergent duality, and we have Sensation in full operation. This sensation involves a *feeling* of diversity (of diverse many totals), and the particular object specifically felt is that object (B) which at the moment most vividly impresses the conscious subject; and B will remain as the object in the field of sensation until exhaustion takes place, or until C or D or E has pushed it out and occupied the field of consciousness for itself in turn. How long the object B may hold the conscious subject in its grip, depends on the extent to which it interests the particular consciousness in whose presence it is. The point of special significance here is that sensation is still feeling in a higher form of reflex activity, that it is *the object which holds the subject,* and that it is successive objects which move it hither and thither. The Subject is subject (in the popular meaning of the word) to the Object. We may now, but only now, talk of Sensation as a phenomenon of consciousness, and we may call that which is sensed the sensate.

Some psychologists tell us that the total object so impressing sense contains or brings with it all the categories. On this see Note A, Appendix. All I would insist on here is, that the sensing of the object involves externality, viz. B *there as extended,* and the feeling of *being* in B.

The sensed total there-being (B) is sensed as a total. This is the sensate. Future experience tells us much more about it. We afterwards find that this total is a confused chaos of particulars, which we call its qualities and relations. But in the meantime we have to be content with the total as a total.

This, however (as I have already indicated), is not all; for the animal and the infant-man *feel* also at the same time the diversity of objects outside, and in a vague indefinite way their localised relations in Space and their successive relations in Time. I say *feel,* simply to indicate that the consciousness of all the other objects which crowd around B is so incipient in its character as scarcely to deserve the name of sensing or sensation—though it truly belongs to this category.

*Note.*—To say that an animal "perceives" an external object in respect of its size, shape, colour, or relations to other objects in space or in time, is to use a term which, in my opinion, is equivalent to *knowing;* and knowing is the distinctive attribute of the man-animal, as we shall see in the sequel.

True, this mere feeling of external objects, as objects and as external, is of every possible degree, and rises to a point of fineness and activity which approaches the borders of per-cipience; but it never crosses into percipience except in a human being. The sensing of external impressions is usu-ally regarded as the basis of such intelligence, intellect, or understanding as each living organism may possess. Intelli-gence in its animal form is simply the reception and arrang-ing of sensates with more or less of reflex co-ordination in consciousness, irrespectively of the feelings or emotions which they excite.

Keeping to intelligence, we find that the animal con-sciousness receives the totalities of objects without distinguishing the parts of these totalities and corre-lating them with the total as inherent in that total.

This, I think, is an important point in the natural history of consciousness. It may be said, how can an animal see or sense the whole of a thing except through the parts? The answer is, that the parts in their totality as a one extended object — *e.g.* a stone — make an impression of a certain kind different from that which another object in its totality makes — *e.g.* a tree.

How, then, can an animal possibly, when it sees a stone for the second or third time, sense that object as the same object as it has formerly sensed, if of the numerous qualities of that object it did not sense a single one, but only a whole in which the single "ones" of quality were all interfused? The answer is to be got from your own experience. You see a man's face as he quickly passes you in the street, and if asked five minutes afterwards, you do not even remember that you saw it; but to-morrow the face you saw yesterday meets you again, and you are at once aware that you saw that same face on a previous occasion, although there was no one part of the face — nose, mouth, eyebrows, eyes, chin — which you could have described even approximately the moment before you saw it the second time and became *then* aware that you had seen it before — in short, recognised it.[1] So, with your eye placed at the hole in the tube, you turn a kaleidoscope and see a certain arrangement of colours and forms in a pattern. You go on turning, and you see the same pattern return within the area of your vision, and you say, "I saw that before." If I ask you which particular thing or things, character or characters, in it are the same as that which you saw before, you cannot tell me *one;* but you are none the less certain that it is the same pattern or a similar one; that is to say, the *totality*, or the *aggregate* of impression, is quite similar to a preceding one, and

---

[1] It is difficult to avoid this word "recognised," though it is a bad one, inasmuch as its etymology points to a prior cognition, whereas there has been *as yet* no cognition at all, but only sensation.

different, consequently, from all the other totalities
of pattern which have been under your eye during
the interval that elapsed between your first seeing B
and then seeing the same B return within the area of
your vision.

Now, an animal does this. A dog does not con-
found the second bone of his experience with a stone.
He feels the similarity with the first bone, although
none of the specific qualities that go to constitute a
bone in sense are sensed by him. No doubt he associates with bone No. 2 a lively sense of satisfaction
arising out of his pleasing relations of yesterday with
bone No. 1; but when I hold out bone No. 2 to him,
his recognition of it as a bone is due to the totality
of the impression being similar to the totality which
constituted bone No. 1.

And I select this illustration because it directs us
to the next point which I wish to note, which is
this —

*Salient Qualities and Impressions.* — While all the
qualities which constitute for the dog the "bone" to
sense are intermixed in a confused total, there probably stands out in relief, after some repetition at least,
one quality which gives rise to a particularly lively
sensation, viz. the smell or the "sweet edibleness"
of the bone. This experience of yesterday with bone
No. 1 stands out prominently as constituting the thing
bone more than anything else does, all the other qualities gathering round this in the confused aggregate
of sensation. There has been an unpurposed selection
of what suits. Plants and animals alike are always

selecting what suits them. The chief, the prominent, the salient quality of the bone is really the bone to the dog, all else being subordinate to the extent of being sub-sensational, by which I mean within *Feeling*, or lying on the border-line of mere Feeling and Sensation proper.

So with other objects. With most objects it is simply the totality B, as not C or D, which has impressed the dog and has clearly crossed the threshold of consciousness, and he senses the totality a second time with a consciousness of sameness or similarity (as the case may be). But with many objects the case is different: there is, *e.g.*, the bone in respect to which one salient quality ("sweet edibleness") impresses him most deeply; again, there is water; again, the specific smell of any object; again, the particular whistle which, when he hears it, calls up into his consciousness the totality in sense which constitutes his master.

*Imitation and Rivalry.* — Again you will notice that if a dog runs at an object, taking it for a bone, other dogs will also run and try to be at the object first, although these dogs, or some of them, may have already seen the object and had not themselves sensed that it was a bone. There is here Imitation. We saw that there was sympathy in the region of the natural feelings; we now, in this incident, see sympathy in the sphere of Intelligence.

And this new phenomenon further reveals a feeling in animals not yet adverted to — the feeling or emotion of rivalry — the desire to outstrip each other.

*Imagination.* — One point more : the image of what
has frequently been present to a dog rises up before his consciousness when it is no longer present.
There is evidence enough of this when he is awake;
much more when he is asleep and dreams that he is
hunting or worrying.   A dog, then, has Imagination,
in its primary sense.

I have led you through this analysis of phenomena
familiar to all, in order to establish the following facts
regarding the sensational intelligence of an animal of
the higher order, viz. —

1. The animal senses a totality without being conscious or aware of the separate qualities which together go to the making of that totality, be it a stone,
or a bone, or water, or anything else.

2. The animal may have, probably always after a
time has, one quality of that totality so deeply impressed on its sensory because of its prominence, or
salience, or some specific relation which that quality
bears to its own organic pleasures or pains, that the
total object is to *it* this particular quality *plus* a
vague and wholly unanalysed agglomeration of qualities which together make a "total single" of impression on his sensorium.

3. The animal senses the likeness and unlikeness of
these totals or objects, *i.e.* it *compares ;* but its comparison is the comparison of sense or sensation, and
is accomplished *on it* by the diversity of objects, not
*by it.*

4. The animal associates one experience with
another; *e.g.* when a dog sees the cook open the

kitchen-door, he has a sensational image of bones, or when he hears a whistling, it calls up the sensational image of his master. The animal, then, has association of sensations.[1]

5. The animal remembers: when he sees A for the second or third time he feels the resemblance to the A of the first time; and, further, the association of A with B tends to call up B out of the storehouse of recorded impressions when A presents itself.

6. The animal has imagination: for it not only retains sensates, but these are suggested to his consciousness when the actual object is not present but merely suggested by association. So also when he dreams, the image of a sensate is clearly before him: the dog hunts in his dreams.

7. Two dogs seeing a bone at the same moment, or one seeing it and the other instantaneously interpreting his excitement, run for it. Animals, then, have sympathy of sensational intelligence.

8. Animals in presence of an object of common desire have a feeling of rivalry — a feeling of competition one with the other, which we may call an emotion, as it is distinct from the desire for the object they pursue.

But all these characteristics of intelligence are in *sensation alone.* The conscious subject is moved hither and thither by the wind of the moment.

---

[1] I shall affirm, without further analysis, that the rule or law of this association is fundamentally this, that things felt together (in space or time), or as immediately sequent, tend to arise again together in the consciousness.

In short, an animal's intelligence is a reflex intelligence. He receives, and, under the stimulus of impression or *recipience* alone, he reacts.

I am aware that the term reflex is generally applied only to *unconscious* response to stimulus in vegetable and animal. I think, however, we need it to mark also a state of *conscious* response to stimulus. Animals are conscious automata.

The impressions of single "totals" made on consciousness, whether from within or without, are, as we have seen, registered for future use. This means that they involve some process in the nerve-cells. Consequently, the involuntary or accidental repetition of the process in the cells (however started) will place the image of the absent object before consciousness. Also, any particular stimulus of the nerve-cells may set agoing a movement in another set of cells in a purely dynamical way, and without any consciousness intervening. This relation of cerebrations, as such, may be held, and yet we may also hold that the particular "*consciousness*" set up by stimulus No. 1 sets up a "consciousness" No. 2, which involves the corresponding nerve change as *its* consequent.

RECAPITULATION AND SUMMING UP. ATTUITION.

By analysing a complex case (the lion-family) we were enabled to collect together the various inner *feelings* in animals; meaning by feelings those states of the individual which stimulate to activity of some sort, and are complete only in activity. These arose either primarily from within, as, for example, the appetites, owing to those necessary workings of the animal economy which we call instinctive or innate (and which we have simply to *accept* as given potencies within the organism waiting to evolve themselves) ; or they were stimulated into existence from without after a nerve-transmission of impressions through the consciousness-capacity of the animal (which we call its intelligence), —the channel of communication with the outer world.

We have now also gathered together the characters of this animal consciousness in its relation to the external. It is mere repetition to say that we have assigned to the animal mind the following characteristics : —

The animal has sensation, and senses as mere matters of fact all that affects its being from within or without.

The animal senses external objects as "totalities" without sensing the individual properties of these objects, still less sensing them as individual properties going to make up the said total object.

In sensing total objects the animal senses them as diverse one from the other. Therefore the animal senses likeness and unlikeness.

The animal senses an object, and when doing so senses its sameness or similarity with the same object as formerly sensed; therefore, the animal has memory.

The animal can sense vividly some specific quality of an object as involved in that object, while all the rest of the said object is in the confusion and mist of its original aggregate so far as sense is concerned. Therefore (and for other given reasons), the animal has association of sensations or impressions, and is under the influence of that association.

The animal, further, through association remembers, and through sympathy imitates, and rivals.

The quantity and quality of an animal's relations to the external world (which external world is to it, as to us, a various and complex chaos of coexistent and sequent series) depends on the constitution of the animal. Some animals may touch the world only at one point at a time, as the sea-anemone and the snail seem to do. Its sensations in these cases are *units*, and very uninstructive to us, though sufficient for the preservation of the animal's own existence. But as we rise in the scale of animal life, we find a more complex constitution bringing the conscious animal-being into wider relations with the complexity of its surroundings; and, above all, enabling it to receive and deal with a sense-totality, a single object as distinguished from other objects, and to have, *simply, however, as sensation*, Comparison, Association, Memory, etc.

To formulate and tabulate: —

ANIMAL MIND OR CONSCIOUSNESS.

I. As regards Intelligence, we have in animals —
1. Sensation of objects.
2. Comparison of the diverse as a sensation (likeness and unlikeness).
3. Sensation of relations of objects in time and space.
4. Association of sensations.
5. Memory.
6. Sympathy of intelligence, and consequent imitation.
7. Imagination.

II. As regards inner Feeling, we have in animals —
1. The feeling of life-activity.
2. The natural appetites working from within.
3. Sympathy of being and of natural feelings.
4. The feeling of kindness to others.
5. The feeling of pleasure in kindness received from others.
6. The feeling of a superior power in presence of anything that may hurt.
7. The feeling of resistance (animal courage).
8. The feeling of fear or of evasion of anything that may hurt (animal cowardice).
9. The feeling of rivalry.

All these insist on manifesting themselves as occasion arises.

We have now before us the mental constitution of the higher animals; but I should not have thought it necessary to dwell on this so long had it not been that we have here also *our own human constitution* in so far as we are animals. Further, we have before us our own nature and limitations up to the age of twelve months, less or more.

The animal is a victim of its own sensations and feelings and associations. It is driven hither and thither by them. It is, both as a creature of inner feeling and outer feeling, merely a bundle of stimuli and reactions or reflex activities. It does not get beyond the reflex action of the cerebrum *and* of the conscious subject, although the constant repetition on its sensorium of external facts, calling for a constant repetition of responses, enables the more finely organised animals to do things, by virtue of memory and association, that approximate very closely to the actions of a rational being; especially when they are in constant contact with rational beings and imitate them.

Now, the stage of Mind reached by the highest animals, whereby they are able to sense a total object, I call the ATTUITIONAL stage. It is the highest form of sensation (the lowest form of which is merely sensibility to a unit of impression), inasmuch as it is sensation of an aggregate of qualities (impressions) constituting *in their aggregate* a single object, and sensed by the animal as an externally existent whole. There is, in truth, a *sensational* reflex synthesis; for which the proper name is Synopsis.

# LECTURE II.

WHEN we speak of educating a man, the question, after all has been said, comes to this: How shall we make a *man* of him? and, in the case of a girl, How shall we make a *woman* of her? We do not propose to make a woman of a boy, nor yet to make a man of a girl. They are different from the beginning, and they are to be as different in the end as they are in the beginning, neither more nor less.

But boy and girl share something in common, and that something is neither the male nor the female element, but the human. Thus far, the aim of education is the same for both; and when we use the phrase, "the education of a man," we use the word man in a generic sense as signifying humanity. The "worthier" gender stands for both male and female.

Now, if I desire to "make a man" of a boy, I do not wish to train him up to be like this man or that man; but to be a true man. My standard of man is not Jones or Brown or Robinson, but the ideal of man. It is something universal, not particular. And this ideal of man must contain the essence or idea of man — that whereby he is *not* anything else, but

75

only *himself;* not a wolf, nor a pig, nor a bear, but a *man.*

Clearly, then, if I am to educate a boy I must have, in my thought the ideal or complete notion (to call it so for philosophical consistency) of a man; not of Jones or Brown or Robinson, as I have said, who are poor specimens enough, but of man universal — of man as not anything else but himself.

Now, in building up the complete notion of "Man," I have already taken the first step, — an important one, too; for I have begun at the foundations of the fabric, and shown you what man is in so far as he is animal. Even as animal, man is richly endowed by nature, of which he is still a part, and with which he lives in the constant interchange of give and take. Simply as an animal, man is the most capable of all animals in the sphere of feeling and sensation. No doubt an animal of one kind develops for his specific needs a keener sense of sight, and an animal of another kind a keener sense of smell, another is fleeter, and so on; but, take him all round, man is a finer, subtler, more enduring, and altogether more admirable product than any animal you can name — in brief, the "paragon of animals."

If we stopped short at this point, then, we should have to consider what steps had to be taken to educate him to be a perfect *animal* of his kind. And, in truth, the earlier races thought of little else, for obvious and sufficient reasons; and even in these days you hear such expressions as this coming with a pecu-

liar gusto from those who have not, probably, in their
heart of hearts got very much beyond the stage of
barbarism, viz. "The English public-schoolboy is a
fine animal."

To pass from this, however, we must admit that if
man were only the finest of animals, our duty as
educators would be to have in our heads a standard
or type, and to educate him up to *that*. We should
not think of educating a cat into anything but the
perfection of its own kind, any more than we should
think of educating a rose into a vine or an elm, but
simply into being the best possible rose. You see
the labour and ingenuity spent on an ox or a horse to
make them the best of their own kind. In short, we
educate a horse or an ox or a rose up to the perfection
of itself; that is to say, up to the *ideal* of an ox or
a horse or a rose, which ideal we have present to our
consciousness in imagination.

All animals and plants have much in common: and
to confine ourselves to animals here, *they* have the
greater part of their nature in common. But each
has something whereby it is itself. A horse and an
ox have a great deal in common: indeed everything
except that which finally differentiates the one from
the other, and makes the ox an ox and not a horse,
and the horse a horse and not an ox. This differentiating "somewhat," which is a secret, but which I
infer from outer manifestations in appearance and
in action, I call the "idea" of the ox or horse; and
if I am to educate either of these animals truly, I
must, while paying due regard to all other facts and

conditions of their existence, specially direct my
attention to the "idea." To this I must educate
them, so that they may be the best of their *specific*
kind respectively. The total conception I have of an
animal is to be called its NOTION, the differentiating
character or characters are the "idea" within the
notion.

Now man is not only the paragon of animals, he is
something more and different. If I am to educate
him aright, then I must, while paying due attention
to all other conditions of his existence, — to the total
concept of him, the Notion, — educate him up to that
"something" which differentiates him, and lifts him
above and distinguishes him from other animals, if
there be any such characteristic. And as this differentiation is a differentiation which lifts him *above*
animals, it *must govern all I do* in educating him as a
whole, because it is placed there by his Creator to
govern all else that goes to constitute him, inasmuch
as it constitutes him what he really and truly *is*.
The idea in a thing always governs, always must
govern and control the parts of the whole; otherwise
the thing would not be itself.

What is that "idea" in the notion man ? Here we
have him an attuitional animal of a very fine sort
placed in numberless relations to nature and to other
animals like and unlike himself, and instinct with all
those feelings, and innate impulses, and sensations,
and connate capacities, which I have already enumerated. But all these feelings and sensations are on
an equal level — in so far as he is an animal. He

gratifies first one then another as the fit seizes him
or necessity demands, just as an animal does. He is
a bundle of particulars; he is without order in himself; he is an anarchy or chaos. Beasts, it is true,
have instincts *to* this or that, or *away* from this or
that, so strong that they manage fairly well to adapt
themselves to their environment, and live and act in
a satisfactory, though beastly, way. But man, alas!
has no such certainty of instinct to guide him, but
has instead an endowment which specifically charac-
terises him — "whence all our woe!" This endowment confounds the natural operation of instinct.

The specific endowment which makes man different
from other animals, lifts him above all animals, and,
consequently, above his own animal nature, is essentially and primarily WILL. If I had asked you for
the differentiating characteristic which constituted
the "idea" of man, you would doubtless have at
once said *Reason;* and you would have been right.
But for the sake of simplicity itself, I beg you to go
deeper down and see in Will the root, possibility, and
essence of this very endowment which in its fulness
is called Reason.

When some speak of Reason as being the specific
endowment of man, they would almost seem to think
that a piece of clockwork had been put inside him,
on the top of his animal mind, to regulate that mind;
and then, when you come to the moral sphere, — the
sphere of conduct, and encounter Will, they seem to
speak of Will as if it were a bare force subsisting on
its own account, and working in more, or (generally)

less, harmony with the clockwork Reason, side by side with which it stands like a sentinel at an "out" barrack's gate.

Now, if you desire simplicity,—the simplicity of truth,—try to get rid of these inadequate conceptions of Reason and Will. If you do, you will attain to a fundamental point of view which will give unity to your whole conception of man as a being to be educated whether you regard his intellectual or his moral relations.

Imagine yourself to be a conscious subject or being such as an animal is, looking out on the world, receiving impressions from it, and having sensation of them and of the various objects by which you are surrounded and to which you are related. You receive these in sensation simply as they present themselves, and you sense and do this or that according as objects impress and stimulate you to reaction. This is the attuitional condition. It is summed up in the words "reflex consciousness."

Again, throw yourself into a rudimentary state of mind, and feel the dreaminess and confusedness of it —the condition in which you are when the brain, exhausted by illness, takes slight note of things, or when, recovering from a faint, the outer has more power over your mind than any inner energy you can bring to bear on it, when the vital centres fail to react, and you cannot distinguish object from subject, and all is dreamily subjective. This would seem to be the condition of a babe in arms.

Better still, perhaps, imagine yourself coming from another and wholly different planet, suddenly planted on a clear night on Edinburgh Castle with the stars above you, the brilliantly lighted town spread out beneath you, girded by a moonlit sea and backed by a misty suggestion of the distant northern hills. You have not had time to recover yourself, your consciousness is overpowered, you are aware of a multiplicity and diversity of objects and qualities; but that is all. Sensation in an elementary chaotic form barely one step beyond Feeling (in which subject and object are inseparable) occupies the field. This gives place quickly to a vivid sensation of this or that particular object, and sub-sensations, or feelings, of all else.

Soon you rouse yourself out of this sensational or attuitional condition, and bring the energy lying within your consciousness to bear on all these sensations. You move out of yourself to seize them one by one, separate one from another, discriminate them as separate totals, and reduce them all to some kind of order — though it be only an order of locality.

Now, this movement, from within your conscious subject outwards, to seize each separate thing by itself and for itself, is to be called *Will.* If any weak person, calling himself a "scientist," has a superstitious dread of the word Will, let him call it Spontaneity.

This state of consciousness is no longer the mere reflex action of animal consciousness stimulated by external impressions; it is that, but it is something *more.* It is the free outgoing of your conscious subject to take possession of these various and varied objects, and make them your own by distinguishing one from the other, and *placing them back* in your conscious subject as your own — re-ducing them to the conscious subject. Along with this act there arises the impulse of *naming.* This is true doctrine unless you accept the only alternative, viz. that the mind of man is to be explained as a bundle of impressions and reflex actions determined always and at all times by something *not himself,* and that what you imagine to be the purest and loftiest act of Will is merely (as some would call it) the resultant of a "complex of sensations." It is at *this* point, and at *no other,* that the battle of Free Will as a moral question must be fought, and either gained or lost. If Will be not root of pure reason, it is an illusion to imagine it free when directed to moral ends.

Now this movement of will, prehending and bringing back, or reducing, to your conscious subject an object which is already in the subject as a sensation (or thing sensed, a sensate), is PERCEIVING or *Elementary Knowing.*

The very word perception — *per* and *capio,* to take — points to the nature of the act as an act: so does apprehension — *ad-prehendere,* to seize to yourself.

Through the evolution of this Will in your conscious subject you have emerged out of and beyond animal sensation in its highest form (Attuition), and are now a percipient being, a knowing being, a man-being, a self-determining being, and no longer a mere victim of the dynamical interplay of feelings and sensations.

*Perception* or percipience, then, is the separating of an object *already in sense* from other objects, seizing it,

and placing it in your own conscious subject as then
and thus *known*, and, in the crisis of being known,
affirmed; and thus urgently demanding a *name*.

To ascertain what it is that you first perceive, you
must go back to the record of attuitional consciousness,
and you will find that you first perceive *totals as totals*
— total objects, diverse one from the other, *e.g.* the
guns, walls, trees, streets, lights, houses, sky, sea, hills.

Now, suppose you fall asleep, outworn and overwhelmed by the multitude of objects that oppress you,
and awake refreshed, you re-perceive these "totals"
and recognise them — the guns, the walls, the build-
ings, and so forth. Remember that merely as an animal you are already endowed with memory, association,
a *sense* of likeness and unlikeness, and so forth: I
pass all this as known to you from our previous
analyis.

Now, if you were asked to specify by what qualities
you recognise this to be a gun, that to be a ball, and
that a wall, you could not name one. You would
simply be able to say, "the *total impression* made on
my sense was that which you call here a gun, there a
ball, and there again a wall." You have discriminated
and fixed each total. Perception is always of the
single. This distinct differentiation of an object is
the reduction of the object to consciousness, in which
act *self*-consciousness is involved, though it does not yet
quite emerge. Of this differentiation and reduction,
affirmation, viz. "that thing is" — is the issue; and if
we go on thinking for ever, our last question will still

be our first question, viz. what *is* the object? Along with the affirmation that A *is*, we have, I have said, an impulse to name A. Without a word to fix the determination of the thing, and externalise our consciousness of it, we should probably have to go through a fresh process every time we saw the same object; and progress would be impossible. The articulated sound fixes and symbolises an accomplished process, which, though it be in a sense repeated every time we subsequently perceive the object, is yet repeated with ease and rapidity by the help of the familiar symbolic utterance.[1]

[There seems to be a general law in the universe that impression completes itself in expression, and that the former is incomplete without the actuality of the latter.]

Conscious subject, as now freely willing, moves about prehending all that comes within the range of the tentacles of sense. Further, the conscious subject, thus spontaneously moving or willing, has, within this movement (Will), an end towards which it moves, and that end, at first unself-conscious and terminating in a percept, is (after a slight experience) knowledge itself as such (a universal). Of this again.

The bringing of the sensate a second time into consciousness as a discriminated and affirmed object, is

---

[1] According to this theory, a deaf-mute, before he attains to the use of manual signs, affirms when he perceives. The affirmation is arrested by the inability to articulate; but there is an accentuation of the affirmation, not only in consciousness, but also physiologically, by an inner movement or outer gesture. The percept is thus in some material way fixed, but always inadequately.

called reducing it to the unity of consciousness, — to that basis which remains a "one" in the midst of endless receptivities and activities.

*Perception, then, may also be defined as the seizing of an object as a total and a single and reducing it, as itself and nothing else, to the conscious subject.*[1]

We have now passed from passive-activity to active-activity. We have got pure Will as the differentia or idea of man as distinguished from other animals. Let us keep fast hold of it as the clue which can alone guide us through the labyrinth of mental evolution, and, by reducing all to unity, give simplicity of view. The "idea" in a thing, remember, governs by inherent right all the elements in that thing. It is supreme in all its relations to the thing, and all the relations of that thing to other things.

We have now passed from Nature (with its impressions and reflex activities) to SPIRIT and FREEDOM.

Note now: 1. The definition of Percipience; 2. That percipience is of *singles;* 3. That it is an act of *discrimination* whereby one is separated from all else — all else being meanwhile in attuent sensation alone; 4. That percipience as above defined is of inner sensates as well as of outer sensates; 5. That the knowledge of all we can finally *know* begins with percipience; 6. That this percipience is the first

---

[1] There is here manifestly a *process* which is a dialectic process; but for this I refer to my book entitled *Met. N. et V.*, merely saying here that this first and elemental process of percipience is the process of Reason generally, or, as we say, its Form, Essence, or Idea.

movement of Reason in taking the universal complex we call experience, and, subsequently, each
individual complex, to pieces with a view to building
up these elementary percepts into a *known* unity, and
so superseding the *sensed* whole, the mere attuit;
7. That after the first act of percipience is performed,
the total sensate or attuit is converted into a percept;
8. That an attuit involves consciousness; a percept,
self-consciousness; 9. That the mere *separation* of
sensates (singles or aggregate wholes) as diverse in
attuition, is a separation effected by reflex action in
response to an impression or stimulus; while the *discrimination* effected in percipience is through an act
of Will, and involves affirmation and speech. But,
above all, note that the movement in percipience is a
*free* movement *of* Will — a differentiating, pure, sub-
ject-generated act which lifts man out of the animal,
and is thus, as idea of man, the key to all intellectual
operations (*e.g.* Concept, General Concept, etc.), the
governing principle in Ethics, the guide in the maze
of Political Philosophy, the master-conception in the
education of a human being.[1]

The educational deduction is this —
THE EDUCATION OF MIND AS REASON IS THE TRAIN-
ING AND DISCIPLINE OF •WILL AS A *power;* AND

---

[1] Not only so; but in an analysis of the percipient process which
lies outside our purpose here, and of the nature of the act as a
differentiating, negating, and determining act, lies the true critique
of knowing, and the explanation, though not perhaps always the
solution, of many metaphysical questions.

SECONDLY, THE TRAINING AND DISCIPLINE OF THE
WILL-MOVEMENT AS A *process* WHEREBY THE CON-
SCIOUS SUBJECT TAKES THE WORLD TO ITSELF AS
KNOWLEDGE.

But, *we live in a Real, not in a Formal world; and
in selecting subjects for education we have to consider
man's immediate needs and duties, while always using
these subjects in such a way as to train and discipline
the Will-Power and the Will-Process.*

I have pointed out that what I first perceive as a
one thing is that which is *already a sensate.* To
ascertain, then, what it is I perceive, I must understand what the sensate yields to pre-percipient sense.
It yields — (a) The consciousness or sensation of a
complex extended total; (b) The consciousness of that
total as *being;* (c) The consciousness of that complex
total as localised out there ; (d) A consciousness of
the spatial relation of that total to other diverse
totals.

None the less is percipience the percipience of a
*one* total sensate. The sensate itself is a complex,
but it is as a fused complex that it is first perceived.

***

### Note on Consciousness and Self-Consciousness.

I have said that a sensate is an object in sensation. It is
only when the inner reaction is adequate that an impression
extricates itself from identification with the subject-con-
sciousness and becomes an "object." The fact and word
"object" brings necessarily with it the correlative fact and
word "subject." Prior to this there is a state of what we

may call subjective feeling, but there is no experienced subject, because there is no experienced object.

Now in sensation I do not in any sense *know* the object. The subject is at this stage merely a basis or point of support for the object. I sense the sensate (object) as a something *not* the subject, but the subject itself is not objectified. The subject is sunk in the lower state of Feeling simply. The subject *senses* the sensate, but it only vaguely *feels* itself. That is to say, the subject is not yet extricated from the whole of being and made to stand out as *itself* a substantive and *specific* being. This is possible only at a subsequent stage of mind beyond that of sensation and attuition, — the stage at which there advances, from within, the energy or force of which I have spoken (call it Spontaneity or Will as you please), and seizes or grips the sensate and takes it back a second time into consciousness.

Note that sense and the sensate, the conscient and the conscite,[1] are already there; but the latter, the sensate or object, is *sensed* as the negation of the subject, the former, *i.e.* the conscient or sensing subject, is merely *felt* as ground, and not, in any strict meaning, *sensed* as the positive of the negation.

But, when I a second time, through a pure act of Will, take hold of the sensate or object, what do I do with it? I replace it in consciousness as an object, and at the same time *affirm* it to be an object there-existent (outside) and not me the subject. In thus placing the sensate a second time into the conscious subject, I affirm all that has been sensed, including negation of the subject, and, further, become aware of the subject itself as that into which I have replaced the object. I *perceive* the object and I *sense* the subject; and have now, further, the power of *perceiving* and affirming the subject when the time is ripe.

For the affirmation of negation is the affirmation of position.

---

[1] If I may use such terms.

Why then do I not say at once that the perception of the
object is also the perception of the subject, instead of saying
that the result is only the *sensing* of the subject? The
answer is that the *potency* of perceiving the conscious subject
by the conscious subject, in other words, self-consciousness,
is certainly now on the field; but the act of perception, let
us remember, involves the discrimination of an object from
all other objects through the negation of those other objects,
and we cannot attain to a clear perception of the subject as
such by the subject, except by an observation of *inner* facts
and conditions, — a more difficult operation than the observation of *external* facts and conditions. Accordingly, the
state of the case is this, that we, as a matter of fact, at this
stage do little more than *sense* the subject as, in a general
way, *not* the object. Mind grows gradually and by infinitely
small steps.

# LECTURE III.

WITH all the celerity that belongs to Mind, the percept of the determined total becomes a perception of the elements in that complex total. The moment the subject is conscious of any separate element in the single total before it (the attuit or sensate), it synthesises that element with the attuit as a one with it. This is the point of transition from Percipience to Concipience.

The attuited object, we have seen, may have some quality so prominent as to impress sense more vividly than the other elements in it (*e.g.* to a dog, the smell of the object); still, this quality is, as yet, simply a sensation. But if, in the *percipience* of the total, I rapidly distinguish in it a specific character or quality, the percept of the total is then affirmed along with its most prominent mark thus distinguished.

And this means that the *Percept* of the total attuit has suddenly become a *Concept* of the total attuit.

Why a Concept? Why not still call it a Percept? Because percipience of the singular or individual *must* precede the consciousness of an object as made up of many singulars. The holding together as a unity of

90

differentiated elements in any total object is *Conceiving* in its strict signification.

I have the whole world present to my consciousness as a sensational attuit and as individual attuits. Each object comes to me as a complex and laden with all the categories; many of which are blazoned on it and simply received by me, such as extensity, quantity, quality, relation; others are implicit, and await the emergence in my consciousness of the capacity to see them, which capacity is a pure activity, viz. Will. All as yet is in sense.

I then make the first step in knowing; for I reduce this that, and the other sensate or attuit to self-consciousness, as discriminated, perceived, affirmed. But the pure activity of Will, just because it *is* pure activity, insists on prosecuting its work of reduction to consciousness, with a view to the ascertainment of the elements, relations, and implications of the thing before me, in order that it may ultimately convert the as yet complex chaotic thing into a rational unity. Finally, it strives to convert the whole world-presentation into a rational unity or cosmos.

In the last word of the Rational alone can Reason ultimately rest. Will, and the process whereby it reduces and harmonises sensation, has its own right to live, as much as a rose or a bird has. It perseveres in its own existence for the fulfilment of its own life. It has a long and difficult task before it; for it has not only rationally to know things, but to actualise its knowledge in conduct in the face of an infinite number

of obstacles and antagonisms.   But this it must do, or
it will die overwhelmed by nature and sense.

I have reached this point, that from among a multitude of objects in sensation I have discriminated, perceived, and affirmed a total object as a total, *e.g.* orange,
I thereupon discriminate the most salient impressions
or qualities; and so, almost before I am aware of it,
pass from percipience to concipience, from self-consciousness of the single or individual to a self-consciousness of that individual as a unity of separate and sepa-
rable elements.   At this point I have a Concept of
the individual —a true synthesis of activity (not of
mere sense) so far as it goes.   The attuit is no longer
merely a total and single, it is a Unity and a One.
Now, still following the same lines, I begin to discriminate, perceive, and affirm other parts or elements
which enter into and constitute the complex orange to
sense.   These I continue to hold together as they exist
outside there together in the object.   But the object
as sensate always remains as a total; that is to say,
the general total impression of the object on sense is
not superseded: it is only, so far, transcended and
explicated.

Let us return now, at the risk of repetition, to the
salient feature of the object.   In sensation-proper, a
dog, when sensing a man or a wheelbarrow, has a
sensate of these objects as totals, the particular qualities of these objects being fused and confused in the
whole.   But after a sufficient number of repetitions,
he becomes aware of one or more particulars as asso-

ciated with the total in sense and distinguishing it:
it may be the general gait or swing of the man, or the
revolving wheel of the barrow. These prominent or
salient characteristics impress him most deeply (make
a deeper dint, so to speak, on his sensory), because
of their prominence and salience. Different animals
will have natural affinities, as determined by their
organisms and needs, for different qualities in a total
thing present to them. These salient qualities are
only associated in sense; not affirmed in percipient
and concipient activity.

Now, in percipience it is the same as in attuition,
but with a difference. In actively breaking up and
discriminating the qualities aggregated in the total,
you will perceive, first, the deepest impression, that
is to say, the most salient quality. The perceived
total, the orange, is, no doubt, *sensed* as distinct in
number and locality and relation from other objects as
a single, but the elements are as yet *in sense alone*, and
not explicated into perception: for this they are wait-
·ing. It is only retrospectively, and after percipience,
that I am able to say that these elements ever were in
the primary complex at all. You will probably first
of all perceive the roundness, and then the yellowness
of the orange, as opposed to other objects which are
not round and yellow. You now are *conceiving;* that
is to say, you are taking together two or more qualities as constituting the orange as a perceived "thing."
Your concept is now a "round yellow thing." Observe
the word thing — the thing being the total sensate (or
attuit), which always persists in your consciousness

awaiting further dissection in percipience, with a view
to a richer and ever richer concept of itself.

Consequently, however many facts I perceive and affirm, these have always a sub-self-conscious reference to
the total in sensation. (*Note at end of Lecture.*) This
orange which I perceive is not only yellow and round,
but smooth, thick-skinned, pulpy, sweet, odorous.
All these percepts, taken together, ere long constitute
the object in knowledge, and are held together by the
force of my Will. The total single in sensation has
been transformed into a unity in percipience, or a unity
of percepts. These percepts are taken together — con-
cepted — and the unity of the perceived object is now
the CONCEPT of the object.

To CONCEIVE ANY OBJECT, THEN, IS TO TAKE TO-
GETHER IN A UNITY THE PERCEIVED PROPERTIES OF
THAT OBJECT. The Concept is a *One in Many.*

So various and infinite are the suggestions of the
universal outside me, that I, as a mind struggling to
know and to use what I know, am driven into a habit
of mental shorthand. When I perceive an orange as
a total thing presented to my consciousness, I, after
the preceding analysis has been effected, also at the
same moment, *conceive* it as a unity; but I do not
rehearse in my mind the series *a, b, c, d,* which make
up its concept. I see a house: what goes on in my
consciousness? This: first, I *sense* the house as a
total object, separated from other totals in space;
secondly, I perceive a certain quality or property, or
qualities or properties, of that house, *e.g.* its con-

figuration, its colour, its door and its windows (one or more of these), and at the same moment I conceive these percepts (take them together), and say "that is a house," and not anything else.   But there are numerous other formerly perceived qualities of a house quite well known to me which never emerge into clear consciousness at all.   They are sub-conscious, and are ready to be brought up to the plane of self-consciousness if I should happen to want them.

Once I have so far analysed the total object in perception, and affirmed certain percepts as in and of it, I cannot, if I would, now *perceive* a house except in so far as I *conceive* it; for there is now more than one element in my conscious experience of the total as a one.

The percepts by which I recognise a house are, doubtless, those which most vividly presented themselves to me in sensation — the salient and most impressive properties (percepts) which came first in experience, and formed a kind of nucleus round which the others clustered.   These not only came first in experience, but, so far as we can see, they come first in every successive experience of the same object.   For the mind, advancing by stages to knowledge, not only assumes the prior stages, but repeats them.   When I see a house and call it a house, I feel, I sense, I perceive, and I conceive.   The ignoring of this fact leads to not a little confusion in psychology.

*Order in Concipience. — Observe now the order in the Concipience of a complex object;* (a) *The most promi-*

*nent and salient qualities are first perceived, and* (b) *these
remain with us as a representative notation whereby we
recognise an object which has been once conceived by us.*

As our experience extends, all our percepts of things
become concepts of things.   As total *single* objects we
*perceive* the sensate as discriminated from other sensates; as a *one* in many, we *conceive* the object in its
parts relatively to itself as a system of parts.   It is a
unity.   After this stage, we never can be said to perceive an old object, whether in presentation or representation, without conceiving it.

The parts of an attuit which we first discriminate
and perceive are, we have seen, the most prominent
and salient: these being the most impressive of the
qualities of the object, they demand the minimum of
exertion for Percipience.   And these salient qualities
we hold in our consciousness *plus* the sub-consciousness
of the totality as impressed on sensation; and these
together constitute the object for us.

This psychological fact yields us guidance in the
Art of teaching, for it tells us this —

*Principle of Method.* — TEACH FIRST THE MOST SALI-
ENT QUALITIES OR CHARACTERS OF THINGS, AND THERE-
AFTER FILL IN, UNTIL THE CONTENT IN CONSCIOUSNESS
EQUALS THE CONTENT OF THE THING OR SUBJECT
TAUGHT.

---

We have now made some progress in our Psychology,
for we have the whole animal intelligence before us,
which is also ours, and, further, two movements of

mind which are distinctive of man, and which are both dependent on the central energy, Will.

---

*Note.* — *The Sub-Conscious.* — Without entering on the general question of the Unconscious, I would remark here:

1. That conscious or attuent activity, being within the sphere of the dynamical, is constantly operative; but that *self*-conscious activities (which are all on a higher plane), when they are intense and concentrated, suppress the merely conscious or sensational solicitations. Where there is no self-concentration, these conscious or attuent solicitations and suggestions occupy the whole field, being granted, when vivid, a certain dreamy admission to the self-conscious sphere. These consciousnesses, which never cross the boundary line of self-consciousness, fulfil a function in the growth of the fabric of mind generally, as regards its material. They doubtless enrich the soil of mind (so to speak).

2. That it seems to be an error to speak of sub-conscious operations; for unconscious consciousness is a contradiction in terms. There may be, of course, cerebration going on which does not rise to consciousness. There seems, however, to be no limit to sub-*self-conscious* operations, which may be going on unheeded by the self-conscious subject when it is concentrated or asleep. Suspend self-concentration, and we constantly become aware of the fact that consciousness as sensation has been going on. Harking back a little, we recall that the "clock has struck without our knowing it" (as is said) — the retrospective perception of a dying sensate.

3. That a knowledge or volition which has been self-consciously achieved becomes, by frequent repetition, a constituent element in the merely conscious or dynamical life. Effort is no longer necessary, and the act, whether intellectual or moral, is accomplished with only a minimum of self-con-

sciousness being present. It is, secondarily-automatic. The product of the higher energy of self-conscious mind would seem to sink down, as a permanent possession, into the merely reflexive conscious sphere of natural action and reaction, and become an integral part of our nature and character.

# LECTURE IV.

RATIONAL intelligence, as we have seen, is the conscious subject freely functioning Will as its instrument in dealing with the multifarious presentations in sensation or attuition. The subject, as functioning Will, is like Neptune raising his head above the troubled ocean to see what is going on, and to regulate and direct. The conflicting waves have, however, dynamical laws of their own, which they are obeying: the sea-god has to accept these laws, and by his will to control them to certain ends. This energising of Will is at once, accordingly, an intellectual and an ethical movement; for an ethical act is simply Will effecting a thought end, which end is conceived, made one's own, and projected by mind, as motive of action.

You will observe, then, that this fundamental conception of rational psychology has, because of its ethical bearing, a very great significance in education.

In psychology as a science, also, apart from its educational reference, the conception is pregnant with

---

[1] See also Appendix, D.

99

results. The most important is this, that it gives a
clue which guides through the labyrinth of mental
phenomena. Fix your attention on this Will, take
hold of it, and follow it as it moves step by step in its
triumphant progress towards the reduction of all presentations to consciousness from without and from
within. In contemplation of this one movement, you
see revealed the fact that reason is essentially a one
faculty, and not an aggregate of many faculties. And
yet, there are steps to be taken by it which must be
taken one after the other, viz. Percipience, Concipience, etc., and these involve prior attuition, comparison, discrimination, analysis and synthesis. The steps
have to be looked at by us in order of time; but, as a
matter of fact, these, and all further, steps are already
contained in the mere knowing of any one object.
This knowing is, in short, a one complex act; but in
order that we may understand it, the act has, as being
a *process* of Will, to be resolved into its parts — broken
up into its elements. When we speak of Percipience,
Concipience, and the further steps of Reason yet awaiting our consideration, we are simply analysing the
complex unity of the act of knowing any one thing as
it may be known. Since these steps are elements in a
complex, they are to be called "moments," in the one
Will-movement or process. But we separate them
logically, and as the first is necessary to the second, so
we place them in a time-order.

Conceive, then, Reason (as distinguished from and
transcending feeling and sensation — the whole sphere
of Attuition) as —

1. WILL-POWER, pure and simple.

2. WILL-PROCESS, with all that it involves.

Do this, I say, and there can be no doubt that, whether true or not, the conception will give simplicity and unity to your grasp of Reason in all its active successive manifestations on the way to its end, which end is knowledge and consequent action.   Once grasp the central thought and your future study is shortened as well as simplified: the theory of the education of man's intelligence is revealed.

To work out fully all that is contained in the above conception of reason, would be to lead you into what is called metaphysics; but it would be also to lead you away from the practical aim of these lectures, which is the doctrine of rational mind in the definite and restricted field of the education of rational mind.   It is evident that if mind grows to maturity after a certain way, the education of mind must follow that way. Method in education means simply a "way"; and the method of educating mind must be the way of mind itself as it grows from infancy to maturity.   Accordingly, the Theory of Education, in so far as it is Methodology, is simply the governing principles of the method of discipline and instruction, as these can be shown to flow from the way mind grows.

You will find, as you go on, that many of these principles have been empirically ascertained, and have received the support of every writer on education, without regard to the question whether they have a scientific basis in the laws of the growth of mind or not.   Our business here is to bring to view the scien-

tific basis, and make you conscious of it; and this is
Theory as distinct from Methodology.

Let me now sum up what we have ascertained as
regards the animal or sensational, and the man or
rational mind and also give definitions.

# LECTURE V.

SUMMING UP AND DEFINITIONS (THUS FAR).

## MIND.

*Intelligence :* Common to Animal and Man.

[The Feelings and Desires of Animals, as collected in Lecture I., Part II., are here omitted, because they fall under the ethical section of the philosophy of rational mind.]

1. Sensation of objects, and a *feeling* of the individual subject.
2. Comparison of objects in sensation (or as sensates): likeness and unlikeness.
3. Sensation of relations of objects in time and space.
4. Memory (involving retentiveness, and a sensation of similarity of a present to a former presentate).
5. Imagination (images of what is not now present), or Representation.
6. Association of sensations as sensations, viz. association of sensations as like and unlike, and as coexistent, or immediately sequent, in time or space.
7. Sympathy with the intelligence of others: consequently, Imitation.

All this is on the reflex or passivo-active plane of
Consciousness.   The animal is moved by the object,
tossed hither and thither by impressions as reflected
by its own subject.   For example, when an animal
seems to be occupied with an object, it does not
"attend" in any true meaning of that term, any more
than it ever "*in*tends"; it is detained by the object,
and what we have before us is a detention *of* the conscious subject, not attention *by* it.   Again, the animal
does not compare or discriminate: objects compare and
discriminate themselves *on* the subject.   The term
assigned to the reflex sensational intelligence of the
animal is Attuition, not Perception, still less Knowing.

### *Man Intelligence.*

All the above passive activities of mind are constantly operative in man, and constitute a great part
of his daily life, which is largely automatic both in
the intellectual and moral sphere; and they occupy
almost the whole field of consciousness in the mind of
the infant and child.

But now, the conscious subject functions a free
energy or power to be called WILL, and the result is a
movement towards the prehension or apprehension of
sensates, and this in successive steps or moments, by
which it effects their reduction to consciousness,
affirmation, and rational knowledge.   Hence —

1. Percipience and the Percept,
2. Concipience and the Concept:

and the other steps in the one reason-movement still
to be considered.

## Definitions.

At this point it may be well to make clear our
terminology, that you may have it for reference; and
the doing of this will give us an opportunity of con-
versationally revising and supplementing what has
been said in past lectures.

*A.* — MIND is Consciousness from the lowest animal,
to its highest man, manifestation.

The fundamental fact of mind is FEELING, and this
is both outer and inner. Mind starts into existence
with a presentation. We can get no better name for
the rudimentary fact than Feeling, whether we speak
of the intelligence, or of the appetites, of instincts,
impulses, or emotions.

(*a*) *Feeling* is to be defined as an indefinite awareness, in which mind as subject is not yet differentiated
from the presentation which is the content of the Feeling, and which may be called the object. There is as
yet, however, no Object *and* Subject. Feeling may
be of the single or of the multitudinous.[1]

---

[1] Some writers seem to have an almost superstitious delight in
exaggerating the mystery of certain phenomena, and the impossi-
bility of fixing them. Not only can this primal mental state be
detected in the young of animals and man, but the most cultivated
man, unless he is wholly destitute of the emotional element, and
lives an exclusively arithmetical existence from which everything
is excluded save what can be numbered and measured, constantly
experiences Feeling as I have defined it. Indeed, it is pretty certain

(*b*) *Sensation* is feeling which, at the continued solicitation of the presentation, has evolved into a feeling of the presentation or content *as separate.* This stage of feeling is sensation. Sensation, becoming aware of a variety of objects, is the sensation of *diversity;* but this is no new phenomenon, but merely a numerical addition to the first sensation, and like it in kind.

We now have, as a matter of fact, Subject *and* Object; but we do not have a sensation of Subject. For this we must manifestly first sense subject *as* an Object, which is, at this stage, impossible. We feel the object as *not* subject (this is sensation); but we do not feel the subject as *not* object. We simply *feel* subject as a vague point of support for object. To sense subject as an object is to be *self*-conscious — conscious of one's own being as a being.

The sensing of the "object" is not simple. There is contained in this consciousness — the being of the object and the extensity of the object, and the thereness or outness of the object.

The organic appetitive feelings we do not at this stage *sense*, but only feel vaguely.

(*c*) *Desire* is to be defined as a feeling from within, so intense as to cause movement and a pressing forward to some object for its own filling or satisfaction.

---

that even the most rational adult has never a clear perception or conception of anything new, without beginning at this point of vague indefiniteness, where subject and object are undifferentiated. This is Feeling in the generic use of the term: it is also *specifically* used to denote feelings which have an *inner* origin.

(*d*) *Emotion* may be defined as desire to satisfy needs outside and above the merely organic and appetitive; *e.g.* the need of satisfying goodwill to others, the need of satisfying the feeling (when "Reason" appears) of the beautiful, of the universal and rational, of the infinite, and of God. All morality and religion are based on primitive needs, and corresponding impulses to satisfy needs through that which is not the subject itself, but something else.

(*e*) *Sympathy* is a community of feeling of one being with other beings (and with the universal of Being), and is the precondition of all emotion (though best defined after it).

(*f*) *Subject and Object.* — By Subject is meant the one permanent conscious entity which receives presentations to sense from whatever source, inner or outer, they come. The Object is the presentation to consciousness, and is to be called the Presentate.

(*g*) The Representate is the name to be given to all objects in consciousness which have been previously there, but which are not *themselves* now really present. It is equivalent to image, but ought never to be called idea, which is a word sacred to a specific meaning.

(*h*) *Analysis* is the taking of a complex whole to pieces; and Synthesis is the putting together again of the parts, and so transforming the "whole" into a "unity."

This involves the self-conscious separating of one thing from another, and as opposed to that other, *i.e.* Discrimination; and *Discrimination* is impossible without an act of will directed against a complex whole.

(*i*) *Will* is the free self-generated nisus of the conscious subject.

(*j*) *Attention* is an act of will sustained with a purpose.

*Note.* — EVERY NEW MOVEMENT OF MIND PRESUMES ALL THE PRIOR MOVEMENTS, AND CARRIES THEM WITH IT.

# LECTURE VI.

## APPLICATION OF THE PRECEDING ANALYSIS TO EDUCATIONAL METHOD.

WHEN we spoke of the Human Body as vehicle of sensation and of activity alike,— the physical basis of Mind,— we showed that it was the first thing to attend to in the education of the young. The first, because the necessary condition of the health of mind, but not the most important. We must eat to live, but eating is not so important as living. We also deduced the lessons which the laws of the body impose on the educator, whether he be a private or public instructor.[1]

We might postpone a similar application of the Doctrine of Mind until we had completed our survey; but it is, for many reasons, better that you should now at this stage comprehend the educational and concrete significance of the philosophical and abstract, so far as we have gone.

*The First Principle of Method*, as deduced from the supreme ethical end of education, is —

TURN EVERYTHING TO USE.

Corollary — *Teach nothing that is useless.*

---

[1] To save space, these were not elaborated, but only indicated.

Passing from this, let us take up in order the various stages of conscious mind. We encounter first of all Feeling, as pre-condition of consciousness-proper.

## *Feeling.*

I. The babe in arms is, in its earliest stages, a creature mainly of Feeling — that state in which subject and object are practically identified. So far as Feeling, therefore, is concerned, the philosophy of mind teaches us nothing as to the education of mind. All we can say is, that looking to the facts that all is always in and through nerve, it is important to a healthy nerve-tissue that we should protect the child from all painful, discordant, or offensive impressions. Calm and placidity, which indicate a harmonious equilibrium of nerve processes, must have some effect on the future mind-life of the babe. Were it possible then (we speak of an ideal state of things) to promote this equilibrium by securing perfect health in the organic functions, and by admitting to the avenues of sense nothing but pleasing sounds and smells and sights, and avoiding all that is sudden, harsh, discordant, and offensive, it would be a good thing. When Montaigne's father would not permit him to be suddenly awakened from sleep, but roused him gradually with gentle music, he was not so far wrong. Who knows but that much of Montaigne's sweet reasonableness of nature may have owed something to this delicate solicitude? Can any one look at the treatment of infants by the majority of well-intentioned mothers

without being surprised that they are so quiet as they
are?  The mothers seem to imagine that if they are
gratifying their own animal affection, the babe should
in some way respond.  Their general intelligence is
too low to understand the dictates of sympathy for
their little charge.  They think of themselves and
their too explosive love, and not of the actual condition and néeds of the babe.  The instinct of animals
teaches us a lesson.  They never seem to meddle with
their young at this stage, save wisely.  Providing for
all their wants, the parent seems to leave the rest to
nature.  Men and women are apt to forget that mere
gushing tenderness for helpless babes is a very cheap
matter, and that true love shows itself, not in ill-
regulated fondling, but in the sympathetic action which
understands, anticipates, and satisfies the needs of the
infant.  Doubtless, mothers and nurses more or less
consciously aim at this.  Let us wish them more
success.

Let us not forget that the whole of mind, including
the essential man-characteristic, is *always there in the
man-child*, waiting for the conditions which make its
emergence possible.  Accordingly, we cannot say at
what specific point a babe begins to perceive, as distinguished from the mere sensing of, objects; but this
is manifest enough that sensation comes first, and as it
is the source of all future *material* of mind (save the
matter and issue of the Reason-process itself — *nisi
ipse intellectus*), certain propositions may be advanced
with some confidence.  There is an order in the development of Faculty.  Accordingly,

If one Rule of Educational Method be more conspic-uous than another (so far as we have yet carried our analysis) it is this —

*Second Principle:* — IN EDUCATING, FOLLOW THE ORDER OF MIND-GROWTH, WHICH IS ALSO, GENERALLY SPEAKING, THE ORDER OF BRAIN-GROWTH.

An old and empirical rule this: all we can do is to point to its scientific vindication. Doubtless we all have to recognise this rule, whether we will or not; and in our attempts (which are constant) to ignore it we meet with signal failure. But, spite of this, we go on believing that we know better than nature and God, and taking advantage of a child's memory for symbolic sounds we impart knowledge (so-called) prematurely — a practice not only useless, but hurtful and obstruc-tive. Take any subject you please, you *must* regulate your action by the principle, or fail. Not only has each age its own fitting studies, but it has its own way of comprehending and assimilating the same study. Take, for example, religion and the idea of God. The man-child is essentially a religious being, and you have to help him in the slow evolution of his religious life. What can God be to a child? He can be something; but what? Whatever He *can* be, He ought to be by your help; but *no more.* And so on with morality and with all intellectual teachings. Find out what things *can* be to a child, and limit yourselves to that, if you wish to succeed. Of this more fully when we speak of applied method, which is the *Art* of education. I would only make one remark here, that if ever you have the mind of an undeveloped adult to deal with (a

Central African, for example, or a British boor), and desire to teach him anything, you must, *even with him*, start from the simplest child-elements of it. (Let the clergy and missionaries take note of this.)

The order of mind-growth in knowing is also the order of the object-growth in completing itself. Not only does the knowing faculty move to its end after a certain manner and by a certain series of steps, in other words, by an evolutionary process; but we may say that the object of knowledge itself by a kind of parallel movement builds *itself* up out of sensation into knowledge. It may be said to separate itself from other things, assume its own percept and concept, and so forth: *A* (tree) differences itself as a percept from *B* (bush) and *C* (carrot). We may look at the growth of knowledge from the side of the object as well as of the subject.

Consequently, we can deduce from the Second Principle these Rules —

Rule 1. *In the teaching of every subject build it up in the mind of the child in accordance with the order of mind-growth.*

Rule 2. *Proceed step by step, and step after step.*

## Sensation.

I shall not at this stage speak of those characteristics of the conscious subject which follow the sensing of an object, viz. retentiveness and memory, imagination, etc., because we have still to consider to what extent these native capacities of all mind (if we may use that term) are effected by the emergence and activity of Will and the Rational; and, consequently, anything I might say now would have to be repeated. I speak here only of the Sensational or Attuitional stage of human intelligence.

At this stage we have the conscious subject here and objects there, which objects as sensed we have called sensates. It is probable that this sensational life is *dominant* (though not, of course, excluding Percipient and Concipient activities) from the age of nine months to about six years of age complete — the period (roughly) of the beginning of the second dentition. If this be so, then the educational lesson is that we should *not interfere with free sensational life.*

*Third Principle:* — Up to the age of six, what-ever else is done let there be no interference with the freedom of sensation, but rather en-courage contact with all forms of existence, and promote the natural activity of the child in every direction.

Sensation is observation of external facts and rela-tions; but this of a purely animal kind. It is not *human* observation. Cultivate the senses, we are told, as if this were the sum of early education. This is one of the results of an inadequate psychology. What we have to cultivate — *i.e.* train and discipline — is Percipience and Concipience. But the universal *basis* of finite mind is sense (sensations of the outer and sensations of the inner), and a broad and liberal founda-tion must be laid if the mental growth is afterwards to be broad and liberal and sound. Some people would make the child exact from the first. The exactness of

Percipience and Concipience is limitation. Let the child alone: let him be the victim of the myriad sensations which pour in on him. The soil may be growing nothing, but it is being fertilised with a view to a future harvest. It is mere pedantry to interfere at this stage, and the result will be, or ought to be, narrow and pedantic. By all means provide raw material for the child, but leave him alone to make what he can of it. By all means give him paper, and pencils, and painting brushes, and colours, and bricks, and spades; but let him alone. We were not sent into this world to be manufactured by pedants, but to grow from our own roots and soil. Nature in this earliest stage is itself accomplishing the work that has to be done for the individual mind. But we can do much to help nature here as elsewhere: and by "helping" I simply mean giving nature a chance and removing the impediments which civilisation has put in one child's way, and giving to another child the advantages of civilisation.

For example, a city child comes into contact with so many existences,— persons and things,— and these for the most part in continual motion, that his senses are stimulated to an early, even precocious, activity beyond the possible experience of a rustic. On the other hand, the rustic is impressed by the comparative repose of things, with the forms of nature, with animals, and the slow operations of agriculture, and so receives a depth of impression which gives solidity, without variety and alertness, to the future intelligence. A rustic child, then, should visit cities for

activity and versatility; a city child should visit the
country for nature and repose. It is not necessary to
be always directing the child what to look at. Let
him *feel* to repletion, and leave "Eyes and no Eyes"
to the copy-books. Let him look at what he likes,
but give him opportunities. This is what I mean by
cultivating sensation. Percipience and Concipience
are, of course, going on in the child, because he can't
help it. He is selecting what suits him; and you may
depend on this, it is not what suits *you*. Sensation,
as such, is the basis of the future operations of reason,
and should be rich and various that it may be fruitful.
Do not, therefore, limit, or in any way restrict, the
receptivity and natural free activity of the child under
the pretext of turning his knowing powers to account.
The Kindergarten system may, as regards the intelligence at least, be abused by the over-direction, with
an ulterior purpose, of the free natural activities of
the child. The chief gain in the kindergarten system
is its full recognition of the activities of the young in
the direction of construction. It thus gives a city
child of wealthy parents, some of the advantages of
the gutter. It is an extension and an evolution of the
nursery practice of playing with bricks, encourage-
ment being, however, given to imitate definite forms
presented as drawings. The flat brick with toothed
ends, admitting of one being fitted into another, is of
more value than all the Frobelian "gifts." The moral
and physical influences, on the other hand, of a wise
Kindergarten are, considering the barbarism of the
lower stratum of our population, wholly good.

And note: what is true of the child is also true of us men. We are (if we may so say) too much the victims of regulated and reasoned sensations, and, consequently, too much the slaves of a narrow and logical activity. We, too, should remember that it is God Himself who so lavishly offers to each of us the riches of sensation and feeling, and that if we do not keep the sensational consciousness open we are guilty of a "sullenness 'gainst nature" and God, and tend to grow narrower as we grow older. Our little personalities shut out the wealth and glory of the universal. We do not wish to rear poets; but except in so far as a man is a sharer in the inspiration of the poetic temperament, he is only half-born. Philosophy and religion are to him sealed books: in the one department, as in the other, he is fit only *jurare in verba* (literally) *magistri.* Reason gives interpretation and form, but feeling is the inexhaustible fountain of reality.

Men, whose avenues of Sensation have been early blocked by the limitations incident to definite knowledge, have often great force within a narrow sphere of intellectual or moral activity; but their narrowness interferes with enjoyment of life in any large sense, and may even unfit them for the administration of important affairs. Their sympathy and imagination are cold and barren. True life, as distinguished from departmental knowledge and purposed activity, includes (always along with these, of course) openness to the universal in all its myriad forms, and a ready response to its never-ceasing solicitations. Education is an extensive as well as an intensive process.

The mind that is the slave of knowledge tends to be
essentially obscurantist, because it is the slave of traditionary conceptions by which it judges all things.   It
is this traditionary spirit which is the enemy of
Humanism, though, strange to say, it is often most
conspicuous in men who have been trained exclusively
in the (so-called) Humanities.   The historical struggle
between Obscurantism and Humanism repeats itself in
every age, and, indeed, in the struggles of each individual with himself.

In the case of the city child, then, let him have the
country as much as possible; in the case of the rustic,
let him have the city: and failing that, markets, fairs,
travelling circuses, panoramas (especially geographi-
cal), musical entertainments, games, and magic-lantern
exhibitions.   It is true that the life of sensation is
never more, intellectually, than the attuition of objects
as wholes and of their relations in locality; but this,
after all, is the foundation of the fabric of mind, and
has to be respected.   But we are not to forestall the
next stage of mind-evolution.

Take note of this, however: just because a child is
a human, and not a mere animal intelligence, the rudimentary acts of Percipience, Concipience, Generalisation, and Reasoning are all going on, in a dim and
groping way, during the whole of the sensational period
without your interference.   For example, the marked
and conspicuous difference of one thing from another
— a stone from a piece of wood, grass from trees — is
making the percipient act, though it is an act of will,
easy.   So with concepts of individuals, which to a child

consist of the most prominent characters *only.* So with generalisations, which are rude and inadequate because they deal only with what most vividly impresses sense. To hasten the ripening of these acts is to barter life for knowledge, and to cheat the child of a multifarious experience which will be afterwards in due time turned to account.

Up to the age of five or six you may introduce a child to new objects as sensational wholes, which in his ordinary experience might escape him; but this is all. He perceives these objects as "wholes"; and object-lessons should never go beyond this. During the last two years of infancy — the sixth and seventh years — you may safely give object-lessons of a more extended kind, but they must be given as an exercise in the perception of qualities which are obvious and superficial; and objects *not* within the range of common life should always be avoided. It is in the breaking-up of what is *already* attuitionally familiar that the discipline of object-lessons consists. There is no good to be got from a lesson on copper ore or on a megatherium. This is a fact of ordinary teaching experience, and confirms the deductions of the theory or science of education. But, perhaps, we somewhat anticipate in these remarks.

When we begin formal instruction, the principle of method to be deduced from the above considerations, which exhibit sensation (inner and outer) as the basis, and as furnishing the raw material, of all subsequent processes of mind, is this —

PRESENT TO SENSE.

The visible must be seen, the tangible must be touched, the odorous must be smelt, the audible must be heard, the inner feeling or elementary emotion must be felt.

## Will and Percipience.

The characteristic of sensation is variety, multiplicity, disorder, even confusion, into the midst of which, as we saw, Will enters in the form of the rudimentary reason-*act* of Percipience. The important, nay, vital point in the movement which we call reason, is this, that it is Will. I can perceive nothing, conceive nothing, *know* nothing, save in so far as I do so as a self-conscious subject that wills. The fact that there is no conscious effort in much of our knowing, that it is so easy to begin with, and becomes, in the course of repetition, almost automatic, does not affect the question. Try to perceive and conceive, or in any way know, something new and strange, like that clock on the wall, which you can imagine yourself seeing for the first time when totally ignorant of its purpose and mechanism, and you will realise to yourself what Will is as an initiating energy, and also what it is in its process.

What principle of method do we deduce from the fundamental fact of reason?  This —

### EVOKE THE WILL OF THE PUPIL.

This principle lies at the root of all true discipline of the mind of man, just as it lies at the root of that mind as rational mind. Sensation furnishes the material and occasion of the new movement, but, at the same time, it blocks the way, and has to be overcome.

It is true, as I have said above, that in the case of a child as of a man, the oft-repeated and insistent presentation of an object in attuition makes easy, and almost unconscious, the movement from within whereby that object is perceived. If, however, I present, even to a child, an object which by its novelty stimulates him to interest, he exerts himself to look at it, and to handle it, and so forth, *i.e. attends* to it, and so perceives it as a total, like or unlike previous experiences; and he then immediately advances rapidly to the *conceiving* of that total through the perception of its most conspicuous characters. The continuous application of will to an object of knowledge with the purpose of knowing, is called Attention. Every teacher fails who cannot in practice solve for himself this problem, "How can I secure the attention of a class?" The general answer is, "By following the principles of method in teaching;" but to this has to be added regard for physiological conditions, and the extent to which the teacher's *manner*, as sympathetic, interested, and vivacious, engages, by a natural reaction, the interest of his pupils.

In teaching a subject, I must follow the process of knowing, whatever that process may be. I cannot advance by walking backwards.

Manifestly, then, in evoking will to enter on the path of knowledge, I must begin with Percipience and go on to Concipience, and so forth. Percipience is first, and lies at the foundation of all accurate knowledge. I find accordingly certain principles here awaiting me. All is complex, but perception is of the single. Accordingly we have this priniciple —

IN THE TRAINING OF PERCIPIENCE CONFINE YOURSELF TO WHOLES AS SINGLES, AND TO SINGLES AS WHOLES.

RULE. — *One thing, or one element of a thing, at a time.*

Let any rational mind try to realise in itself an adequate knowledge of any new thing whatsoever, and he will fail until he has analysed the complex in consciousness down to its underlying percepts, and distinctly apprehended these.

It is no mean element in the work of rational mind, this accuracy of Percipience. It is the foundation and necessary condition of every subsequent step, if that step is not to be simply a step into confusion.

It may be of little moment to perceive distinctly the object "tree" as opposed to "shrub," or any one quality in tree as opposed to any other one quality in tree, so far as mere substance of knowledge is concerned. But the important point in this, as in all other educative processes, is the training and discipline of faculty. This has always to be kept in view as our main end, — *effectiveness of faculty;* and we can then let knowledge take care of itself. This *is* education of intelligence. Nothing else can be called education without involving ourselves in a contradiction of terms. One percept at a time, then, and that clearly differentiated.

## Concipience.

The next step in knowing an object is the raising of the percept of the object as a single whole, to its perception as a unity. Mind has been discriminating diverse objects one from another. It now continues its occupation with each object to see what the object has got to say for itself. The various qualities impress themselves on sense, and have now to be discriminated in relation to the total object, and as elements in it; and those qualities which are not obvious have to be sought for.

The mind in knowing will not be hurried. It must take one step after another, and only one at a time. Like all things in nature, it grows by infinitely small steps.

In teaching botany to a school I present a bluebell. To the children it is familiar; but it is little more, as yet, than a perceived attuitional total. If they know anything about it beyond what they know about all other plants that are becoming daily familiar to sensation and perception, it is that on the top of a thin green stalk there is a blue cup. To this extent the bluebell is not only *perceived* as a whole in sensation discriminated from other things, but is *conceived*, by virtue of certain qualities and characteristics of its own, relatively to itself.

It is manifest that until Will, in the energy of knowing, has reached the point at which it discriminates the various characters which go to make the complex individual in sense, it has advanced only one step beyond attuition, and that the second step is the truly instructive one.   It is now answering the question, What *is* that complex object before me? — the first and final question of reason.   The answer is ascertained by an analysis, which gives an adequate, though, of course, superficial, synthesis of the elements in the object; and this synthesis constitutes its (unity in many) concept.   Will has here a higher and more difficult task to perform than in Percipience, and greater demands are made on its sheer power of *holding things together*.   The discipline of Will and the training in the process whereby Will reaches knowledge, are here, accordingly, higher than they have yet been.   It follows the prior discipline in simple percipience.   Consequently the principle —

In training in Concipience practise in the synthesis of one in many.

But remember, meanwhile, the magistral principle of *order* in conceiving, and confine yourself to the obvious for a considerable time.   Not only must you confine yourself to the obvious for some time, but in your first exercises you must limit yourself to the most *salient* characteristics.   Why?

Because we discovered in our philosophy of mind that it was the salient characteristics which were first apprehended by mind in building up a concept of a thing.   Thus a second principle (not to be called a rule, because it is not a deduction from a principle, but itself directly deduced from the mind-process) —

IN TRAINING TO ADEQUATE CONCEPTS OF OBJECTS, TEACH FIRST THE SALIENT AND PROMINENT CHARACTERISTICS BEFORE PROCEEDING TO OTHERS.

Anticipate a little, and apply for yourselves this principle of method to geography, history, grammar, language generally, etc., and you will see how sound it is, and how universally it is neglected.

No doubt a human being, especially if he has a happy nerve-basis and a suitable environment, may do much of all this for himself; but if he could do it as well as he ought to do it, education, whether by the parent or the teacher, would be superfluous. It is because the human animal cannot educate himself that we interpose and educate him. And, so far as the intellect is concerned, it is only by following the method of mind in its process of knowing that we can teach any subject effectively, or as Comenius would say, easily, solidly, and surely. But far more important than the teaching of particular subjects is (let us never forget) the training and discipline of the knowing function in man. Reason (which is sometimes called divine) is in our hands, to make or mar. Our responsibility is great. For on reason and its sane activity in search of true knowledge, depends ultimately the true ethical life — the life of conduct as well as of contemplation.

Far be it from me, however, to say that, without the

formal training and discipline of reason, a man cannot be ethical. He may be so constituted as to have a natural affinity for the humane feelings which are the fountain of the ethical, and he may be by nature so open to the spiritual ideas which are presented to him in the example and teaching of others, that he leads an exemplary life in all his relations. God has not left the all-important question of conduct in the hands of intellect alone. Even "to the poor (in mind) the gospel is preached." But we cannot trust to such casual results. The very purpose of all education is to strengthen the ethical in the individual, for himself and for humanity, by the discipline of reason, at the same time that, by that discipline, we secure a more effective discharge of all the duties of life, individual, social, and political. Surely a great work! An uneducated man, moreover, however finely attuned by nature, necessarily has narrow interests: his horizon is limited, and he must always fail to rise to ethical conceptions in any large sense. The world and all its interests are for him his village and his home.

It may be said by the hypercritical, that, after all, many of these principles of method, so far as we have yet gone, are already in the market. True; but they are not bought and paid for by those who most need, and ought to use, them. Experience in the course of the ages forces profound truths on men with the very minimum of thinking on their part, simply by showing them that certain things won't work and certain others will. Nature, so to speak, takes care of itself; for there is a Reason in the affairs of men. Our business is to explicate that reason, and to find the scientific or rational explanation of good practices, and to show the untruth and ineptness of bad ones. This in education is called theory, and it is this which every man who proposes to educate a mind is asked to study.

# LECTURE VII.

## THE GENERAL CONCEPT.

THE process of mind on its way to knowledge has been our theme; but our work is as yet only half done. The moments of sensation, of perception of sensates, and the conception of the percepts inherent in the complex sensate, take us a considerable step on the reason-road. We can imagine an intelligence so constituted as to stop at this point; but if so, its reduction of the material in sense to self-consciousness, and consequent knowledge, would be partial and inadequate. The concept, even supposing it complete, would give us only the separate parts of a single thing in unity. These are in the object fused, for we cannot locally separate the colour from the form or hardness or. odour: they are not separated parts of the thing standing side by side as a collocated aggregate. Still they are collocated parts of an aggregate in the sense of elements in the total thing. We may regard them as the *anatomical* description of the thing. But we are not content with this as knowledge.

We press forward to a higher conception — the conception of the relation of these parts, which *relation* truly constitutes them into the actual thing before us. Passing over many subordinate and preliminary analy-

128

ses, we ultimately desire to *see* the molecular elements
of the thing, and the dynamic force or forces which
bring about that specific constitution of molecular
elements which we call the "thing." The mere collocation of parts gives us no satisfaction; we desire to
detect the precise nature of the energy which determines that these elements shall be here A and there B
or C. In short, we seek the causal relations of the
elements within the thing and "for itself."

For, after all, the question we ask of each thing
(and of the whole of experience) is, What *are* you?
You have qualities which I find everywhere else: your
colour I find in other things, your texture and hardness and odour and form I find in other things; but
they are combined in you in such a way as to make
you a thing by yourself, and not anything else. And
I want to know what you truly *are* — in short, what is
your essence, which is also your idea, and the purpose
or τέλος of your existence.

To face me, I have a quantitative difficulty: Will
is a great power; it can hold present to consciousness
several percepts and concepts at once, while, at the
same time, more or less vaguely sensing a multitude of
subconscious or sensational elements which can be
made to emerge when I desire to realise them clearly. ·
But the multitude of individual concepts is so great
that Will exhausts itself quickly in their presence,
and gladly catches at some way of symbolising many
individual concepts as represented by one. Millions
of dogs are represented by the one word, "Dog" or "a
Dog"; millions of individual men by the one word,

"Man" or "a Man."    We say "a Dog is a quadruped,"
meaning "all *dogs;*" Man is rational, meaning "all
*men.*" We thus abbreviate the work of Will-reason.
This is itself a great gain if it were nothing else,
because it abbreviates and simplifies thought.

[To this aspect of the general concept I mean here to
confine myself. Its relations to Cause, Essence, Idea, lie
within the sphere of metaphysics.]

If we can utter a judgment the predicate of which
will cover at once many millions of individuals, it is
manifest that we have acquired an intellectual sym-
bolism which facilitates enormously the progress of
reason in knowledge.

How then do we get for consciousness the word
"Dog" as distinguished from this, that, and other
dogs?

Thus:

I have already perceived and conceived an individual object, differing from other creatures within
the area of conscious experience, and named it "dog."
Many other creatures now pass before me which,
though differing in certain respects (which are superficial enough), *e.g.* size and colour, are yet possessed
of those characters which made me originally call a
particular creature a "dog" in order to mark *it* off
from the many other creatures previously seen. Because they possess in common those characteristics
which difference a dog from other creatures, I call
them all "dogs." While doing so, I am gathering up,
by the force of Will, into a unity in my consciousness

these common (differentiating) characteristics, and so constituting a new reality (for consciousness), the kind, species, or genus, or class, Dog. This is the General Concept which manifestly exists as an entity of Reason only; its actual existence being found only in that series of individuals in which I have noted the common characteristics. "Dog" is all dogs and no dog.

*General Propositions.* — Now this General Concept is the mother of general propositions, thus: The common characteristics, above referred to as found in the series of individuals, are *a, b, c, d.* Consequently the general concept Dog contains in itself, ready to be explicated whenever I choose, the general propositions —

All dogs have *a.*
　　　"　　have *b.*
　　　"　　have *c.*
　　　"　　have *d.*

Note next, that the affirmation of the general concept "Dog" presumes that I have seen all individual dogs and recorded their characteristics. But it is in no man's power to do so. There is, then, manifestly lying buried in the general concept "Dog" an assumption or hypothesis, viz.: This dog, that dog, and a multitude of creatures (to which I originally attached the differentiating name of "dog") represent or stand for "all dogs;" *therefore,* "Dog," as a general concept, contains all dogs. So firm and rigid is the conviction that I have got the true general concept which exhausts individuals and affirms a class or kind, that if any traveller sent me a picture of a strange animal and called it a dog, I should say at once, "It is not a dog, *because* though it has *a* and *b* and also a certain general sensational resemblance, it has not *c* and *d*, and is *therefore* not a dog, but some new beast not yet classified.

[Some may say that the general proposition must precede the general concept. Doubtless it is silently there, but in its explicated form as a proposition it follows (I think) the general concept, and is an explication of it. For educational purposes this matters little.]

The formation of the general concept, apart from its value as the shorthand of reason, is of great significance. It implies a *power* of Will in discriminating and holding discriminations together in a unity, with a sub-reference to innumerable individuals, much greater than any yet brought into operation. The abstraction necessary in percipience and concipience is here quite outdone; quantitatively outdone, and also outdone because in holding present to consciousness the general concept, we have now no longer the support of the thing as there and then present to consciousness, but, instead of this, only an entity generated by mind.

The significance of the General Concept is great, because it carries with it the whole process of reasoning or ratiocination as distinct from Reason in its larger sense: and in reasoning are included both Induction and Deduction.

Its importance in the ordinary life of man is also great; because the true measure of our power over things lies in the truth of our general concepts. On this the accuracy of our judgments in the affairs of life depends.

Its ethical importance again is supreme; because the general concept is the "form" of ethical ideas, and these constitute at once the motive and the end of all conduct.

Further, the importance of a proper understanding of the process of formation is also great; because, if understood as it has been explained above, ethical ideas, however exalted, are not in themselves existent, but are existent only in so far as they make manifest their existence in the particulars of conduct — the daily and hourly life of each of us. They *live*, they can truly *live*, only in the particular.

You can understand, then, how it is of all things most desirable that in the self-education of our own minds, and the education by us of other minds, we should see to it that they are trained and disciplined in the accurate construction of general concepts. On this depend soundness of judgment and the validity of concrete reasoning.

A treatise, *De Emendatione Intellectus*, might well centre round the general concept. Not only for its own sake, but for its implications; for this stage of the process of Will in knowing rests on the previous stages, without which it could not emerge; and it contains also implicitly the ratiocinative function. Without the accurate concept of the individual, which, again, depends on accurate or true percepts, and these on full and true presentation to sense, the general concept would be hopelessly vitiated: and the vitiation may enter at any one or all of these stages.

*Principle of Method.* — TRAIN THE YOUNG IN THE FORMATION OF GENERAL CONCEPTS, AND IN THE ANALYSIS OF THOSE THEY HAVE IMMATURELY FORMED. With this object in view obey the following rule: —

RULE. — *Teach generalisations as generalisations; that is to say, proceed from the particular to the general; from the concrete individual to the abstract.*

The tradition-bound teacher of language will say that the abstract syntactical rule of grammar can be learned quite easily by boys. Of course it can — as *words;* but it can never be anything but a meaningless collocation of words until it is filled with the concrete individual "instances" which the boy is daily encountering in his studies. And inasmuch as the human mind, as a matter of fact, gets its general and abstract proposition (even if it has to do so retrospectively, *i.e.* by going back) through particulars, our duty is to lead it to its general proposition along the road or way of particulars. The mind will thus make easier and more solid and more rapid progress in the knowledge of a subject, and will also have an intellectual interest in the subject. But these are not the sole, nor yet the chief, advantages; for it is only by following the *way* of reason that we can truly train and discipline reason to the sound and effective exercise of its powers on all the affairs of life.

The same remarks apply to the teacher of elementary

science. Even the humblest school-science consists of
generalisations, or aims at them. Unless the pupil is
led, step by step, to approach these through particular
observations, full and exact, the conclusion, be it in
the form of a generalisation or a formula, is not knowledge any more than the case which contains a diamond
is the diamond. The great facility many boys have
in appropriating the words and propositions that formulate knowledge, deceives the teacher. *Real* contact
with *particulars*, so that the boy himself can of himself draw the scientific conclusion, is alone of any
value. Even an unintelligent knowledge of a Greek
verb is more disciplinary and more instructive than
verbal scientific knowledge. Such knowledge is not
*real;* and it is only in so far as it presents the
real relations of things, and in so far as these are
clearly perceived and conceived, that science instruction has any rightful place in the school. The
Ratichian rule, "per experimentum omnia," is here
absolute.

And yet words and formulation are necessary. If,
without the help of language to fix and symbolise, we
could make little progress on the percipient and concipient planes of mind, how hopeless would be the
attempt to convey a generalisation and reasoning without it. Until we formulate thought to ourselves in
words, we are not, strictly speaking, thinking, but
only striving to think, struggling with thought —
"licking," as Montaigne says, "the formless embryo."
On this parallelism, or rather interpenetration, of
thought and language, rests ultimately all argument

for language as an educational discipline; apart, that is to say, from its ethical and æsthetic aspects.[1]

*Note.* — Here I may state explicitly what I have elsewhere indicated, that the child — indeed, we may say more truly, the infant — begins with general concepts. By this I merely mean that the infant, having seen and named an individual (the totality of impression which is the individual in sense), forthwith uses that individual image and name as a general. Having once seen and named a cow, he calls the four-footed animals which thereafter come before him "cows," until he knows better (as we say).[2] So vague are sensates, and the first percepts of these sensates, that he sees a general likeness before he begins to differentiate in any close analytic sense. Till he gradually, by the concurrent processes of differentiation and likening, builds up for himself the concept of this and that individual, he is constantly wrong, and the resultant in his consciousness is always confused and inadequate. Still more must this be the case with the process of forming the general concept, which demands much more energy of will applied to things than the individual concept does; for he has to compare, analyse, and discriminate with a view to the integration of a new unity in consciousness. Not only is this process one demanding in itself more energy of will, but it is vitiated by all prior errors in

---

[1] Dr. Sully (i. p. 420) refers to a deaf-mute who, before learning the manual signs, reached "the highly abstract idea of Maker and Creator, and applied this to the world or totality of objects about him." If my analysis of percipience in *Met. Nov. et Vet.* be correct, this is not impossible. He had the *feeling* of Being-universal, and the perception and conception of the multiplicity of objects as grounded in Being-universal.

[2] Why does a child see generals vaguely, and only slowly advance to differentiation and true generals? Because he is in the sensational stage, the victim of impression, whereas the analytic act is an act of Will directed against the object, and is necessarily of slow and gradual emergence.

percipience and concipience — nay, also, by the incomplete-
ness of the primary sensation. Concepts both of the individual and of the general are allowed by the inactive mind
to form *themselves* (so to speak) as vague impressions, and
the result is fatal to adequate and accurate thinking. We
educate in order to correct all this. We do not, however,
wish to interfere too much with the natural flow of mind,
but only to regulate and direct it; and, as the young grow
older, we further wish to rouse in them a self-conscious
*purpose* of attaining a knowledge which shall be exact and
true.

The next movement of Mind in knowing is Reasoning, Inductive and Deductive, already contained in the
general concept, but now explicit and self-conscious.

Having treated this briefly, we shall then speak of
Cause as ground of things, just as Reasoning contains
the ground of conclusions.

# LECTURE VIII.

REASONING OR RATIOCINATION — MEDIATE
AFFIRMATION.

WE now have to deal with the final processes of Reason, viz. Reasoning, and the ascertainment of the Grounds or Causes of things.

As I am not attempting a systematic treatise on Psychology, but rather exhibiting, in lectures, the critical movements of the conscious subject in reducing the world of sensation to itself, I shall take the privilege of a lecturer and briefly repeat, though in a slightly different form, what I have already said on general concepts, because a consideration of these is, it seems to me, the best introduction to the reasoning process.

Think what an unfortunate gift the power of acquiring percepts and individual concepts would be if we stopped there. The whole complex world would be an infinite series of individuals. If we, as endowed with Will, felt an impulse to go further, memory would break down. You could not speak of "hill," or "dog," or "cow," but only of certain individual objects one after the other, each with its own specific name.

138

As a matter of fact, individual things outside are all in community with other things, and share their properties. The fire is hot, so is the sun; the grate is black, so is a negro's face or a starless night sky. Many animals are so like each other that we popularly say they are the same animal; not numerically, but yet the same, *e.g.* one cow is like another. There are slight differences of size and colour, it may be, but they are substantially alike (whatever "substantially" may mean); and we apply the same name to all of them, though as individual objects there are hundreds of millions of them.

This is, as we have seen, GENERALISING, or the forming of GENERAL CONCEPTS; grouping individuals as kinds or classes.

When I speak of a cow, *e.g.* in this way, "The cow gives milk," "The cow is good eating," and so forth, I do not specify in thought or speech any particular cow more than another, but all cows whatsoever. Thus, under cover of one word used as a symbol, I am able to speak of millions of things.

Now, how do I get at this admirable time-saving, thought-saving result?

Thus:

I have perceived an individual cow: nay more, I have conceived it; that is to say, I have perceived certain qualities which it possesses, and these qualities — *e.g.* living, animal, four-footed, cloven-hoofed, large-uddered — are grasped together as a unity or concept in my mind, which reality I have called a "cow." But numerous animals pass before me, and

I perceive such a resemblance of qualities in certain
of them that I feel that they are not only similar
animals, but substantially the same, though numerically distinct. All these similar individuals I call
cows; and then I find that I can talk of cow, or "the
cow," in a general way, meaning all cows, but yet no
one particular cow more than another. This thing of
which I speak is the cow as a *class* or *kind*. The word
cow is now no longer simply an individual sense-
concept, but a GENERAL CONCEPT, and the name "cow"
is a general or class name.

Now, what have we been doing? Evidently com-
paring one animal with another. That is to say, we
have held present to consciousness certain individual
sense-concepts, and looking from one to the other we
have seen likeness or unlikeness, and have gathered
under one general, or class, or kind-name, all the
similars.

This is COMPARISON. *Comparison, then, is the basis
of generalisation.*

The general concept cow is reached by us after a
comparison of a large number of individual or particular concepts. Looking at a great number of animals
which are *prima facie* like each other, we have found
a common expression for them — which common expression I call a general concept. Spite of many
differences, each animal has certain qualities *a, b, c,
d; therefore, a, b, c, d* are the common characters, and
any word may be the symbol of these.

There is, manifestly, in this process a high energy
of will as a sheer power holding things together; and

that, without the advantage of a sensible support as in the sense-concept.

But this general concept "cow," though it is one word denoting a unity of particulars, contains implicitly the general proposition, "All animals called 'cow' have *a, b, c, d.*" The general concept then contains in it and yields general propositions, which have for their sign the word "all."

In saying "All cows have cloven feet," I merely say out at large what already had been put by me as the result of my perceptions into the general concept "cow." "Cloven-footed" was one of the qualities or characters which we, on comparison, found always present in a certain number of individual animals, and was one of the grounds for our throwing them altogether under the name, class, kind, or general concept "cow." It is as if I had put ten pebbles into a bag, one of them red, and then said, that bag contains ten pebbles, and one of them is red. I knew what I put *in,* and so I know what I shall take out.

Many difficult and subtle questions arise in common with this generalising operation.[1]

Enough for our purpose to note that I have reached the general proposition, "All cows are cloven-footed," "All cows are large-uddered," "All cows are ruminant," and so on, by perceiving these several char-

---

[1] For example, as to the complex of qualities which constitutes the general concept cow. A gentleman arrives from the Antipodes to show me a cow which has solid hoofs like a horse. Another arrives from Spitzbergen to show me one which has a thick coating of fur, and so on, and so on. I shall pass this question here (advisedly).

acters in each of the animals presented to me, and
which I have classed as cows, or rather, under the
general concept and name "cow."

It is thus, as we have seen, through the perception
of the particular or individual that we reach the general
proposition, and that the general proposition has
meaning to us — is alive to us. If we do not see the
general proposition, in and through its particulars, it
is simply so many words — *voces et præterea nihil.* Of
this again in a minute or two, under "Induction."

As to Comparison : — We said that animals were able
to *compare;* but it was the comparison of one *sensa-*
*tion* with another, — a vague indefinite process on the
plane of sensation, and also very restricted for want
of Will to separate, to perceive, and to hold percepts.
They *sense* likeness and unlikeness of objects. The
likeness and unlikeness is imprinted *on* them. But
they make no further progress, because they cannot
function free Will: consequently, they do not perceive
and conceive objects; that is to say, *know* them by
separating, seizing, apprehending, and placing them
back in their conscious subject, as a thing taken possession of and labelled. What enables the child to
shoot ahead of the animal and perform this process?
Will, and nothing but Will; a free movement issuing
from the conscious subject, which spiritual dynamic
constitutes his differentia, and enables him to advance
and to conquer. By dint of this Will he perceives
and affirms relations, and also the fact of relation as
an abstract. By this he holds each percept or concept

close to him, and perceives (not merely feels) the differences. The holding of two or more objects close
to consciousness in order to perceive their likeness or
unlikeness is, we have said, COMPARISON. But it is
no longer now the comparison of animal sensation, —
a mere feeling, a comparison made by the thing (so to
speak) *on* the reacting conscious subject, — but the
comparison of perception and conception, — the comparison in which Will, the conquering energy evolved
in the conscious subject, plays from first to last the
leading, because the conditioning, part. It seizes the
qualities which are the common characteristics of individuals, and holds them apart from the individuals.
This is the Abstraction of generalisation.[1]

*Note.* — But before going farther, let me point out that
while the above is the order of the process whereby general
propositions are first reached, it is for the most part an
unself-conscious operation. The forming of percepts is unself-conscious, the forming of concepts is unself-conscious,
and the forming of general concepts and the general propositions implicit in them is unself-conscious. By this I mean
that we go on doing all these things, in the first instance,
without any set purpose, but only under the general stimulus of Will-reason. But man being a self-conscious being,
can become aware of his acts and propose to himself deliberately to perform these acts, with a view to knowing things.
For example, I become through sensation aware of a great
many objects which, though somewhat differing, yet, roughly

---

1 No dog or horse can speak at all, or name even one quality;
still less can either of them say or think, "All cows have cloven
feet." And yet, I think it by no means impossible that certain
sounds should emanate from animals as *associated* with certain
*individual* things.

speaking, may all be called "grass": and I may deliberately
proceed to collect all these objects and endeavour to find out
what they have in common. And after careful observation
of each of the different, yet similar, grasses, I come to the
conclusion, "All grasses are *a*, *b*, *c*, *d*," etc. One differs
from all the rest in respect of *f*, another in respect of *g*,
another in respect of *f*, *g*, and so on, but they all have the
qualities *a*, *b*, *c*, *d*, etc., in common. Thus I reach a general
proposition purposely and self-consciously.

The object of psychology of the Intelligence (in which
is necessarily included the fundamental principles of logic)
is to bring into view the various operations which mind
carries on in order to reach knowledge or truth. Thereby
we extend knowledge itself by a knowledge of that which
is the organ of knowledge; the most interesting, surely, of
all objects of inquiry to the being whose differentiation and
prerogative it is to know. And besides this; by revealing
the process we stimulate to the correct use of that process,
and guard ourselves against prevalent and almost inevitable
abuses of it; for the human mind is always packed full of
generalisations, a great many received from parents and
others — all of them provisional, most of them quite wrong,
and leading to endless errors of opinion and conduct.

The lesson to be drawn by the teacher, as I have
already said, is this, that general concepts and generalisations are mere words and nothing more, except in
so far as the particulars are known: this is essential
to their being distinct and clear. In other words, let
general concepts and general propositions be taught
in the way in which they are formed.

The transition to the next movement of mind is best
made, I think, through a consideration of the act of
judging.

*Judgment and Deductive Reasoning.* — From the very first we have been judging — always judging.

To judge is to predicate one thing of another. But even in the first percept ever formed by us, we affirmed the identity of a thing with itself. Judgment is also affirmation, which, when put in words, we call a proposition; *e.g.* "a horse is a quadruped." The first limb of the proposition we call the Subject, and the second the Predicate.

Every successive movement of mind is by way of judgments; for of everything, whether it be a percept, a concept, or general concept, we say that "it is," or "is not."

It is unnecessary for our educational purpose to go farther into the subject of judgments. Indeed, the subject is introduced here only because it seems to be the most natural and easiest approach to the apprehension of the process of Reasoning, or the Syllogism. For a large number of our judgments are *mediate* judgments;[1] that is to say, they acquire truth and validity, not by the direct perception of the fact before us, but through other judgments. I am referring to those judgments which involve general concepts. For example, I say, "This tree is an oak," without realising to myself the ground of my affirmation. If I realise that the ground of my judgment has been the observation that it produces gall-nuts, it is at once manifest that my judgment is mediate or syllogistic, and when explicitly stated is this:

---

[1] All judgments are at bottom mediate; but to show this would lead us aside into metaphysics (*Met. Nov. et Vet.*).

All trees that bear gall-nuts are oaks.
This tree bears gall-nuts;
*Therefore*, this tree is an oak.

These three affirmations, propositions, or judgments we call the major premiss, the minor premiss or subsumption, and the conclusion.

Thus, in a multitude of ordinary colloquial judgments, we are always syllogising without realising that we are doing so.

The process which has been illustrated above is mediate judgment, or reasoning, or ratiocination, or the syllogistic process (deductive). If a traveller in Central Africa writes that he met with a strange animal which was yet to all intents and purposes a cow, then I know that *that* animal must have the qualities $a$, $b$, $c$, $d$, etc., which he and I, and the rest of us, have agreed to regard as constituting a cow, as distinguished from every other animal. I then proceed thus:

All cows have $a$, $b$, $c$, $d$, etc.
This new animal is (I am assured) a cow;
*Therefore*, this new animal has $a$, $b$, $c$, $d$, etc.

Or, you may ask me the question, Has a new animal lately found in Central Africa cloven hoofs? I say, What does the traveller call it? You answer, He says it is a cow. Then I reply, It has cloven hoofs; because cloven-hoofed is one of the qualities which, we have agreed, go to constitute the animal cow. Thus:

All cows have cloven hoofs.
This new animal is a cow;
*Therefore*, this new animal has cloven hoofs.

*This is Deductive reasoning;* and its truth depends on the truth of the general proposition under which you conclude as to this or that predicate of the individual which you range or subsume under the general proposition. You are simply taking out of the general concept or proposition, in relation to a particular case, what you have already put into it. You see then how careful men must be of their general propositions, which, in truth, are mostly wrong; and even when they are right enough for colloquial and provisional purposes, they are wrong scientifically.

Your syllogism may be in point of *form* quite correct, but if your general proposition is defective, to that extent your particular conclusion is defective and *really* incorrect.

How then did we get this general proposition on which so much depends?

*Inductive Reasoning.* —Here we must go back to the general proposition (p. 141), "All cows are cloven-hoofed," which was extracted out of our general concept "cow," the moment we had made it. There was here a secret process going on which has to be brought to light.

We had been gradually noting, as was pointed out, the qualities which we might predicate of an animal called a cow to justify us in calling other animals "cows," and not horses, or anything else. Among other things we noted "cloven-hoofed" in each individual animal that passed before us. Then the general concept cow yielded at the very moment of its formation the proposition, "All cows are cloven-hoofed." We might not put it in words, but the proposition was silently there, contained in our act and the conclusion of that act. And it was so contained because we had examined, one after another, a large number of instances. We had virtually said this animal, which impresses us in such or such a way, *we* call a cow, and it is cloven-hoofed. Cow No. 2, which similarly impresses us, and which we also call a cow, is also cloven-hoofed, and so on. And then we concluded, "All cows are cloven-hoofed."

Now, had we seen all cows? Certainly not. Accordingly the process was this:

> This cow, that cow, and the other cow have cloven hoofs.
> These cows which we have observed represent all the cows not yet observed;
> Therefore, *all* cows are cloven-hoofed.

This process is evidently the same as the syllogistic process whereby we affirmed confidently that the cow in the African desert was cloven-hoofed, simply because it was a cow, and because all cows are cloven-hoofed. But it is the reverse process. It is a mediated *general* judgment, mediated through particulars. It is a process whereby we reach the general judgment or proposition through particular propositions or judgments. *This is Inductive reasoning*, and is the process by which we formed the general concept, in the formation of which inductive reasoning was implicit.

Thus reasoning (syllogistic) goes inductively from particular to general, and also deductively from generals to particulars; and the concluding judgment, whether particular or general, is always *mediated*.

Thus by means of these general propositions as *induced* from particular propositions, and by means of particular propositions which may be *deduced* from them, we acquire a kind of mental shorthand which gives us great power over our materials of perception and conception, and enables us to connect things together in a reasoned whole. So strong is this impulse of rational mind that its ideal aim is always a reasoned system of things — a cosmic connected whole.

But we have always to be on our guard, because our general proposition may be on wrong lines. It may be defective in its particulars, to begin with. Such general propositions, in truth, are always provisional in their character, and to that extent have an arbitrary look.

[It is only when I am able to name the qualities which a cow *must* have in itself to be a cow, the qualities "essential" to a cow, that I am entitled to say that I have truly a right to a general proposition which is irrefragable. And this "essence" I cannot get hold of. Yet enough is given me for the ordinary purposes of life and knowledge.]

Now, at this point we might, as finite intelligences, rest satisfied. We can reduce the multitude of objects by which we are surrounded to percepts and concepts: we can determine their relations, and gather these together into general concepts and general propositions; and further, we can move freely from one thing to another, and arrange all our knowledge in a convenient way, as a connected rational system. But this does not suffice: there still awaits us the final and consummating movement of mind — the mediation of the *real;* or Causal Induction.

Before considering this final reason-movement, let me again impress on you the bearing of these discussions on educational method. The proposition, "Grass is a living organism," in so far as it is the conclusion of a deductive syllogism, is entirely dependent on the prior general propositions, "all plants are living organisms," and "grass is a plant." The proposition is manifestly analytic, for it is already contained in the general concept "Plant." If grass be an entirely novel experience to me, all that I have to ascertain is whether it is a plant or not, and then I know the rest. This is, as we have seen, what is called a mediate knowledge or mediate syllogistic judgment because it is not direct but mediated through another knowledge, viz. the general proposition. Now, the world and human affairs and relations are excessively complex, and, in order to save ourselves from over-pressure by particulars, we are always taking refuge in general concepts and general propositions. It is evident, then, that if we are not excessively careful in forming our general concepts and propositions, we shall fall into endless error, — error, too, of a particularly fatal kind,

because, the *logical form* being correct, we are apt to
stand by our erroneous conclusion as also *really* correct.

For, as I have endeavoured to show in the specific
educational reference, these general concepts, and the
general propositions issuing from them, are, in truth,
inductions. That is to say, they are the tying up in a
bundle and labelling of a large number of particular
percepts and concepts. The general concept and general propositions, as such, thus give us no new knowledge as regards the particulars (though they may seem
to do so), for each individual percept and concept is
*presumed* to have been seen by us; they merely give
us *this* new knowledge, viz. that all the particular
things are the same, or similar, in certain respects.
Neither the inductive result, accordingly, which is a
general, nor the deductive result, which is a particular,
proposition, give us any *new* knowledge of things
beyond the fact that certain things not within our
immediate purview are alike in certain respects. The
syllogism, in truth, whether inductive or deductive,
is simply a way of first formulating and then utilising
knowledge already presumed to be gained by the
observation of particular things. Accordingly, the
truth of every judgment and proposition, whether it
be a general or a particular, depends, *ultimately*, on the
*exactness* or truth of our individual percepts, concepts,
and general concepts; and it is, consequently, difficult
to exaggerate the educational importance of exactness
in percipience and concipience. There is a mediating
process of mind which is universally recognised as
adding to our knowledge,—a mediation not through

propositions, but through realities,—the mediation
of Cause; but the truth is, that if we trace any proposition whatsoever back to its origin, it too exhibits
*real* relations, and, only in so far as it does so, is it of
any value.

The formation of the habit of exact perceiving and
conceiving is necessary, not only as a foundation for
sound reasoning, but also to enable us to detect in a
complex presentation or statement the important vital
points.   Our knowledge is advanced by bringing new
cases under already known generalisations.   Accordingly, in a new case, we have to detect in the object
before us those characteristics which, spite of its
apparent novelty, bring it under some general concept
or proposition through certain attributes of likeness.
This demands an active and penetrating observation
of its various features.   A man who can see his way
to an accurate mediate judgment, by bringing the new
particulars before him under some general head, is
said to be a man of sound judgment.   To judge soundly
is one of the highest functions of intellect, because it
involves accurate discrimination and perception of the
elements in the thing before us, the possession of
general concepts which are in their content clear and
distinct, and thereafter the power of relating the particular to the general with a true insight into similarity.   The man who can do this supremely well in
science, philosophy, or politics is the man of genius.

In the ordinary affairs of life, again, the man who
can readily detect the characters, more or less hidden,
of the particular case before him, and bring it under

its solving universal, is the prince of practical men.
But it is not always an easy task.   A man may cultivate a solemn expression, and have always the air of
pronouncing sound judgments, and may thus easily
acquire a reputation with undiscerning people as a
man of "common sense."   But the reputation is constantly ill-founded.   The men who "look wiser than
any man ever was," are often to be distrusted.   Sometimes they are not truly in earnest in their desire to
get the truth, but merely to play the *rôle* of judicially-
minded men, and they will consequently, after due
shaking of the head, utter a common-place which
solves nothing.   They are ambitious, not of truth,
but of a "reputation."   Then, again we have men of
honest and truly sound judgment; but this within a
very limited range of principles.   Their area of vision
is circumscribed, and they unconsciously hasten to
reduce the particular question before them to one or
other of the few formulas which constitute their stock-
in-trade.   They are to be respected as the necessary
ballast of society.   A judge on the bench is thus arti-
ficially limited, though, personally, he may see beyond
the law-inscribed horizon.   The truly sound judgment
on the complex before a man will be found to be, for
the most part, predictive.   It is justified by the sequel.
And this remark applies, not only to ordinary affairs,
to commerce, to politics, and ethics, but to scientific
investigations.   For such a judgment there is needed
the greatest possible exactness in matters of fact,
truthfulness of purpose, and, above all, a regulated
imagination.   The *issues*, both in the sphere of pure

knowledge and of action, are always present to the supreme judgment.

Educationally, then, it is difficult, as I have said, to exaggerate the importance of exactness of mind. It is also clear that a man cannot be called educated in the highest sense, unless his education has been directed to this end of sound judgment. The education must be not only intensive and exact, but extensive in respect of the material of knowledge. But both combined will fail to produce the educated man, if there be not the ethical impulse and the ethical aim; so closely are the intellectual and the ethical interwoven. There must be a *purpose* of truth.

In teaching, then, the endless affirmations or judgments current in ordinary intercourse and in literature have to be traced to their general ground (or as it is sometimes called "principle"), and not accepted simply because they are *as propositions* clear and intelligible. If a man does not carry on this process while reading or conversing, he is the victim of endless fallacies. Accordingly, we have to call on the mind we are educating to analyse what is before it, to justify it, and to vindicate its truth by making explicit its premisses, and so reconstituting the synthesis for itself. Herein lies the training and disciplining of ratiocination; and, when we do this, we find ourselves thrown back on percepts, and individual concepts, and wholly at the mercy of these primary acts of intelligence which lie at the foundation of the general. Reality is truth, and truth is reality. All reality is derivative, save the primary percepts.  Thus, let me repeat *ad nauseam,* there is forced upon us at this stage, as at all stages of education, the supreme value of exercise and discipline in accurate discrimination — not with a view to knowledge, but to a habit of mind.   And it is solely because certain studies promote this (*e.g.* object-lessons and science-lessons), that their place in the school can be justified; not because of the knowledge they give.

*Principle of Method.* — TEACH REASONINGS AS REASONINGS; THAT IS TO SAY, ANALYSE THE AFFIRMATIONS BEFORE YOU, AND MAKE EXPLICIT THEIR RATIONAL BASIS.

[Analysis and (syllogistic) synthesis.]
*Analytico-Synthetic.*

# LECTURE IX.

THE proposition or judgment, "Fire burns wood," is said to be a causal judgment. And so it is in a sense. But as it is a mere observation of the sequence of two events, the former of which controls the appearance of the latter, I would prefer here (in view of educational applications) to call it a dynamical judgment.

Now, the whole range of statical and dynamical judgments, even were it within our grasp, gives us only a superficial and preliminary knowledge of things. The central impulse of reason is towards the affirmation of the ground or cause of things. The issue of reason is an answer to the question, What *is* A, or B, or C? and the "is" involves Cause.[1] The dynamical judgment does not satisfy us; for it is a mere observation that one appearance always follows another.

The true causal knowledge of a thing is the compre-

---

[1] When I see a thing in its identity of cause, process, and end, I know it, and, so far as *it* is concerned, there is nothing more to be done. I would fain rest: and, in point of fact, I would then lie down and rest, were it not for the infinite relations of the said thing, and the ultimate cosmic question which is always luring on Will-reason in its free and unresting activity in search of an absolute synthesis.

hension of the how and why of the sequence; and to this all other knowledge is merely preparatory. This kind of knowledge is by way of pre-eminence called Science, *Scientia,* or *the* knowledge. This search for causes of visible existences, results, or effects, is the task of the man of science in all the departments of human experience and endeavour, and not in physics alone.

We feel that we truly know a "thing," only when we know it in its cause or *causes.*

That tree, for example, I perceive, conceive, connect with its general concept "Tree" and its higher concept "Plant," and, through generalised propositions within whose sphere it falls, I can reason to this or that conclusion about it. For example, I do not see its roots; but I know it has them. Why? Because it is a *tree.* I do not see its fruit; but I know it has, or will have, it. But what I now want to know is, what are the causes which underlie the visible, and bring about stem, branch, leaf, and fruit? Until I have ascertained this, I do not really *know* the tree. I am not yet at the end of my quest. Why does that branched object before me bring forth fruit? You answer, "Because it is a tree." I reply, not so; that is the reason why *you say* that it brings forth fruit.

The true cause lies somewhere in the reproductive necessity of the tree's nature. Suppose I could name this cause and call it *A.* A is the cause of the fruit-bearing; but even of this as the true and necessary cause of the fruit-bearing I cannot speak with confidence until I have further ascertained *how* it does it.

It is necessary to see the *process* at work, and we shall then see what the sequence which we call Cause and Effect *must be*.

How do I proceed ?

There are many events that precede what I see. I examine these, separate one from the other, and, carrying my observation through a number of instances, and excluding first this antecedent as the cause, and then that and the other antecedent, I finally isolate the true cause; and, by further examination and experiment, I confirm what I have detected. This is a process of analysis resulting in the synthesis of cause and effect, which synthesis now constitutes for me the true knowledge of that particular thing. It is an analytico-synthetic process; but it is also a process of induction, because I examine numerous "cases" in order to find the truth. I pile "instance" upon "instance," and I also conclude with a general proposition, saying, "All things which are precisely similar to this experience before me are caused in this particular way (uniformity of nature)." And, at this point, enters my previous generalisation of objects into trees, or more generally still, plants; and I say with confidence, "All plants grow thus; if they do not, they are *not* plants."

In ascertaining the cause of the visible thing called fruit, you examine many trees which produce fruit, but you do this simply because you thereby see similar objects in differing circumstances. I take advantage of the experiments (so to speak) which nature makes; and, if nature gives me no ready-made experiments, I make them for myself, as in physics and chemistry:

but this, if I had clearer and subtler vision, would probably not be necessary. One "case" would then suffice. As a matter of fact, however, and as a substitute for my limited vision, I go from tree to tree, observing closely and applying my tests, in order to discover the cause; or to verify what I think I have already discovered. At bottom, however, I have simply been analysing or taking to pieces the complex system of antecedents which have for their invariable sequent, fruit, eliminating what I ascertain not to be the true efficient antecedent; and this I do until I have isolated the true antecedent or antecedents which being present, the result or effect appears, and which being absent, it does not appear.

Having done this I then (as has been said above) take advantage of my previous operations in generalisation, and say, "All fruit is produced by like causes." Why? Because "all fruit" is simply a gathering together in thought of a great many individual things which are already known to be *repetitions* (it may be with slight differences) of the same thing.

I may now put the process in another way:—

We generalise the statical qualities of things. But when we seek the cause of anything, we look at it not only dynamically, but as *grounded* in its antecedent, and necessarily arising out of that antecedent. You regard B as an event which is brought about by some antecedent event. There is a sequence. The antecedent may be *a, b, c, d, e, f,* etc. You have the thing or event B before you, and you put it into ever so many different circumstances, and detect *that* antecedent circumstance or event which never fails to appear, while all the others are sometimes there, sometimes not there. You fasten on this common permanent antecedent among many variables, eliminating the variables, and isolating the common antecedent as the Cause, which we shall call $a$. You can then very often test your results by putting $a$ into operation, and seeing whether B follows. But, although you may be convinced of the necessity of the causal connection, you can never *see* it, until you see *how* it is that $a$ *must* produce B. Your concept or synthesis of B is now $aB$. There are a great many false causal connections current in the world. The function of Science is to reveal the true and necessary.

In ascertaining the necessary causal antecedent of any thing or event, it would appear at first sight that there is no inductive generalisation, and that the term "induction" is incorrectly applied. And we can easily understand that, if possessed of greater intellectual power of perceptive discrimination than we actually have, we should be able to separate or isolate the true causal antecedent of any result by merely looking at the single experience before us long enough. But, *even then*, the process, however apparently intuitive, would be as follows: the cause is not $d$ nor $e$ nor $f$, but it is $a$. It is the function of genius to seize quickly, and almost by a kind of intuition, the true cause. But even genius, and still more manifestly the ordinary investigator, is always generalising. For he looks at $a$, $c$, $d$, $e$, $f$, etc., and sees how each behaves.

Now, this is equivalent to looking at a series of similar cases, and finding what is, among many variables,
the common antecedent fact present always. Isolating
that, he calls it *a*: *a* is the cause of B. The investigator has thus generalised from the observation
of instances the common invariable antecedent, and
causal event.

The process, then, whereby we find the cause of any
existence or change is, I think, rightly enough called
a process of induction and generalisation, although
the fundamental movement is one of analysis and
synthesis.

You will now see that the generalisation which
yields a general concept and general propositions, *e.g.*
"All horses neigh," is an induction of statical facts.
The induction which yields the causal antecedent of
an existence or event is an induction of dynamical
facts or sequent movements, which are *determining*
movements, *e.g.* "Heat consumes wood." We have
been seeking for a *common* cause of a great many *like*
particulars. Whenever there is a conjunction of heat
and wood we now know what is to happen. But,
further, we have not satisfied the causal impulse of
reason until we have ascertained *how* the antecedent
works so as to make necessary the sequent. We thus
get the true and final causal synthesis of the two
things.

*Note.* — This causal conception completes the knowledge
of a thing. In the mind-process, in so far as rational, it is
the primary form of knowing the particular in its most
elementary stage, and it is also the final and ultimate form

in which we grasp the total of things — a One Cause out of which all differences emerge — the unity in all difference. Until the intellect reaches to this conception of universal causal law as explicitly present to consciousness, it has not completed its education, for it does not know God in the world. The religious idea is the final aim of the education of the rational, as well as of the ethical, in man.

*Principle of Method.* — COMPLETE INSTRUCTION THROUGH CAUSES; FOR THE KNOWLEDGE OF A THING IS COMPLETE, AND INTELLECT CAN BE SATISFIED ONLY IN THE APPREHENSION OF CAUSE.

Remember, however, that all educational method is governed by the principle which requires us to follow the order of the growth of mind (which is also the order of the growth of brain); [1] and, consequently, that the age at which a boy is to study things in their causes is a question to be anxiously considered.

Mere dynamical relations of sequence, however, are among the earliest experiences of mind, and the causal in this superficial sense may be early introduced into education. Again, one element in the causal conception is purpose — the use which any concrete thing serves; and this, being always concrete and obvious, may also be early utilised for educational purposes. The superficial aspect of cause I would call, for educational purposes, the relation of sequence. For example, in an early object-lesson on tea, I speak of tea and its uses; but ere long I may extend these sequences backwards to the place which yields tea and the way it comes to us, etc.

---

[1] See Lect. XI. seq.

Even when we have made up our minds as to the age for beginning strictly causal or *science* studies, we must bear in mind that sense and the concrete, and percipience, and concipience comparison must always have their claims satisfied before we proceed to abstract conceptions. And, accordingly, all science teaching which is not a series of experiments and essentially heuristic, is simply word-teaching and charlatanism. A so-called cause may be to a boy merely one more fact, which is of no more significance for discipline than a second aorist, and of little significance for knowledge, save in so far as it is *experimentally ascertained.* I should say that (setting aside exceptional boys and exceptional teachers) a boy cannot begin to study scientifically with advantage even the elements of physiography and of plant-knowledge till his fifteenth year. The preparation for this will be found in object-lessons which have to do with percepts and concepts, and relations of an external and sequential character merely. When he passes beyond the explanation of the facts of everyday experience, he, even at this age, wastes his time.

# LECTURE X.

SURVEY OF THE PROCESSES OF REASON IN ORDER TO
SHOW THAT THEY ARE EACH AND ALL ANALYTICO-
SYNTHETIC IN THEIR CHARACTER.

*Principle of Method.* — TEACH ANALYTICO-SYNTHET-
ICALLY.

This, as resting on a *generalisation* of the nature of
each successive step in mind activity (the will-process), is a *governing principle.*

See Appendix, Note D, for the materials of this lecture. To introduce the argument here would weight
the text too much.

164

# LECTURE XI.

## UNFOLDING OF INTELLIGENCE; OR ORDER OF INTELLECTUAL GROWTH IN TIME.

THE successive stages or periods of mental development from infancy to maturity have now to be considered. "*L'esprit, non plus que le corps, ne porte que ce qu'il peut porter,*" says Rousseau. And again, "*Laissez mûrir l'enfance dans les enfans*"; to which we may add, "Let boyhood ripen in boys, youthhood in youths, and manhood in men." Do not anticipate.

We shall find that these periods pass into each other, and can only be roughly marked off. (See note at end of this lecture.) Speaking generally, the *time*-order is indicated by the *logical* order of the successive movements of intelligence in knowing, as these have been exhibited in the preceding pages. If we regard the logical movements of intelligence, as also the chronological, we, manifestly, simplify things very much.

The successive movements may be roughly arranged thus : —

1. Babehood — The period of *Sensation* and *Attuition* (one year).

2. Infancy — (*a*) *Perception;* (*b*) *Sense-Conception* (from the second year, when speech begins, to the

eighth year, the period of second dentition); (c) *Relational Conception*, including superficial dynamical sequence, and involving crude Comparison and Judgment. The whole of this period corresponds to the duration of the *Infant School*.

3. Childhood — *Conception* (single and relational) is now in full activity with *Generalisation and Reasoning incipient* (from the eighth to the fifteenth year, the age of puberty). This period corresponds to the duration of the Primary School, and is divided into two parts — the Lower Primary, from the eighth to the twelfth year, and the Upper Primary, from the twelfth to the fifteenth year.

4. Boyhood and Girlhood, or the *Juvenile* Period — *Generalising and Reasoning Stage*, when the perception of true *Cause and Effect* becomes active (from the fifteenth to the eighteenth year). This period corresponds to that of the *Secondary* or *High School*.

5. Adolescence — *All the faculties in full operation, and with the further tendency to form ideas,* and to co-ordinate knowledge into the unity of science (to the twenty-second year). This period corresponds to that of University life. Thereafter Manhood and Womanhood.

———

*The Physiological relations of this Development of Mind have to be considered.*

———

The principle has already been laid down that all education and all instruction,— intellectual, moral,

and religious alike,— if they are to be effective, are to
be carefully adapted to the stage of mental development which the pupil may have reached.

*Note. — Transition from one plane of Mind to another.* —
Perhaps this is the place to point out, once for all, that as
all things in the universe are related and interrelated, and
one state of a thing passes into another state by insensible
degrees — degrees so infinitely small that they elude us; so,
Mind is a complex one, in which every element and capacity
and possibility are present at once, and that all our analysis
is merely an attempt to discriminate phenomena that shade
off into each other, in so far as they can be detected to be
distinct and discriminable.   But, all the while, the synthesis
of the whole is always present in each diverse mental manifestation.   We speak of Feeling, Sensibility, Sensation, Perception, Conception, General Conception, Reasoning; but at
what point and in what circumstances are these not *all* present, and at what point does the one pass into the other in the
synthesis of the whole?   No man, it seems to me, can say at
what point a mind that already senses, has entered on percipience, concipience, etc., any more than he can tell at what point
a bud is a flower.   [And yet we are not entitled to say, " All
is becoming "; but rather, if we are to be accurate, " All is
at once becoming and become."]   By extensive observation
of minds, animal and rational, and much self-reflective vigi-
lance, a thinker may put his finger on distinctions; but
when it comes to the actual working of the mind, we can
distinguish only in a very general way.   Take, for example,
the state of " dispersed attention," as it is called.   I should
call this state one of sensational or attuitional dreaming, in
which *I* am carried on from image to image by the play of
mind and the interactions of nerve-cells.   But all the while
I am a man, and, consequently, Will is there lying at the
heart of the chaotic series, and ever and anon striving to
assert its own right to existence, and to mastery over the
objects that entrain me.   At any moment this Will may

press its way through, and my attuitional state become a percipient and rational state. So with an infant. To the age of nine months he may be regarded as an animal pure and simple; and yet he is something else, for Will lies concealed there seeking its opportunity and gradually forcing its way to the front. The eye and face of an infant already reveal that, while he is a victim to sensation, he is yet gradually bringing a reserve force into the field. Then, if Percipience be elemental reasoning, it may be said that he reasons even before he can talk. And so on. All the while, the infant is undergoing the parturient labours of self-delivery. He is bringing forth *himself*— he is not brought forth. The conscious subject is gathering, in silence and in secret, the energy which will soon proclaim itself as Will, and in full Percipience take the first step in *self*-consciousness. [This Percipience is the first movement to reduce the sensational world to a cognitive world, and the process is a dialectic process.]

# LECTURE XII.

## MATERIALS AND DYNAMICS OF THE BUILDING-UP OF THE FABRIC OF MIND AS A REAL.

WHEN B is presented to A (the conscious subject), and A is aware of it (I pass over rudimentary "feeling," of which we can know little), we call A mind and B the presentation. But, further, Mind being the subject of the presentation, we call B the object.

Whether from within the body or from without the body, the access of presentations is through nerve-tissue, and the reactions are also through nerve-tissue. The terminal of the impression is Consciousness, and the reflex return starts in and from consciousness.

The nerve-tissue (which may be summed up in the one word *cerebrum*), inasmuch as it is matter, obeys the laws of matter, and as vehicle of consciousness, receptive or reactive or active, is probably the highest department of physics. Whatever the laws be whereby the nerve-cells transmit movements and maintain communication with each other, and subsequently repeat for themselves, under some inner stimulus, past movements when the existing agent (the object) is absent, I say whatever these laws may be, it cannot be doubted that they exist. As a system these laws would be

109

called Cerebral Dynamics, or the Dynamics of cerebration.

As might be expected *a priori*, there is little doubt that there is unceasing cerebration without consciousness as a concomitant.[1] At a certain point in the process, and under certain conditions, cerebration passes into consciousness.

That cerebrations exist and affect each other, and, without the presence of fresh stimuli, set up in the subject a consciousness which is neither the *a* of primary impression nor the *b*, but a resultant and complex *c*, is not incredible. The dynamics of cerebration we leave; for little is known about it, and inferences are unfortunately drawn from that little which fill the "non-scientific" and merely metaphysical mind with amazement.

It is with the action of the environment (including the cerebrum as part of the environment) when it passes into "consciousness" that we are concerned.

Here we find a mutual involvement and reciprocity of mind and cerebrum. Cerebration sets up a consciousness, and consciousness of mind sets up a cerebration. It is not a molecular disturbance of nerve-cells which causes a dog to seek water, but the consciousness of thirst which results from that molecular disturbance, and which sets in action the whole motor system.

And yet, even in this region of mind, we are still within the sphere of natural action and reaction.

---

[1] Appendix B.

Mind has as yet no inhibitive or regulative energy. The appearances of this regulation in instinct are the result of certain innate impulses, concrete aptitudes, and reflex activity combined. If this be so, then there is such a thing as the natural dynamics of conscious mind traversed by the dynamics of material cerebration.

The next stage of Mind is distinguished by the advance of will and consequent self-consciousness, which profoundly modifies the dynamics of conscious mind and of cerebration, and directs all to ends. This is Reason.

Accordingly, I must ask you to go back to the lecture on the intelligence of animals, in order that you may there see how the instruments of mind, as not yet a self-conscious mind, constructs its own intelligent life. We find in the animal the whole dynamic of conscious mind; and having also found it in ourselves as the platform on which Will and self-consciousness stand, we have to note to what extent the natural dynamic is modified by the intrusion of Will and self-consciousness.

*Natural Dynamics of Conscious Mind as Intelligence.*

We found that the dynamical movements might fairly be generalised under the following heads : —

*Conscious Mind.*

Attuition.
Sympathy of Intelligence.

Imitation.
Imagination.
Association.
Memory.
Comparison.
. Sense of relations in Time and Space.

By means of operations dependent on these factors, the animal mind builds itself up, and the man-mind does the same, in so far as it is animal. As in infancy and childhood the animal predominates, the consideration of these connate capacities or faculties [1] ought to yield much that will guide the teacher to principles of method and rules of procedure.

I cannot, within the limits assigned to this book, treat adequately of these capacities; I shall only give a single brief paragraph to each, chiefly that I may engage your interest in the modification which the emergence of Will effects. These paragraphs will be more fully expounded in lectures.

Generally, it has to be observed that all the characteristics of mind which we share with animals are emphasised and accentuated by Will-reason, and by the purpose of thinking and doing which belongs to Will-reason alone.

## (1) Imitation.

Were it not for the sympathy of intelligence binding creatures of a like kind together, and giving rise

---

[1] It seems to me to be quite unnecessary to abandon the use of so useful a word.

to Imitation, each would have to begin from the beginning for himself, and the growth of mind in each
would be slow.

The recognition of this fact gives us a very important principle of method in education, viz. —

### PRESENT A GOOD MODEL.

This principle is of wide and various application,
and touches the teacher's work in every subject, and
in all his relations to his pupils.   The child naturally
imitates: but, he also *wills* to imitate.   The action of
others supplies him with his concrete ideal.   Note,
however, that imitation rests on *sympathy* of intelligence; and, accordingly, the pupil who by bad management finds himself in antagonism to his teacher
will not imitate him, or, at best, he will confine his
imitation to mimicking.

### (2) IMAGINATION.

This is simply the reproduction in sensation of the
impression made by an object which is now no longer
present.   We thus repeat and revise our sensations,
and are not left entirely at the mercy of objects in
actual presentation.

(*a*) On the plane of sensation we have merely

*Representative Imagination.*

(*b*) When Will-reason enters, we have          ·

*Productive or Constructive Imagination.*

Here the will seizes representations, or images dynamically arising, and even searches for images with a productive purpose.

The principle of method which this yields is —

### CULTIVATE THE IMAGINATION.

And this we do by allowing free play to the representative imagination (a child educates himself even by dreaming), and by evoking the productive imagination,·through the furnishing of the child with productive work, as in fairy tales, narratives of events, simple poetry, and so forth. All this is necessary to the rich growth of mind as a substantive reality; and this quite apart from its ethical importance.

### (3) ASSOCIATION.

#### 1. *Association as Condition of Knowing.*

Sensations and sensates occur in experience either together or in sequence, and they are thus linked together. There is an external linking in time and place, and there is also an inner or *real* linking of likeness and unlikeness. We desire to reproduce past experience, and we have to take advantage of these actually existing dynamical relations. They go on in spite of ourselves, it is true; but the introduction of Will-reason enables us to take advantage of them with a view to recall past experiences for purposes of knowledge. Association as an instrument in the building up of the fabric of knowledge is a subject demanding from the psychologist elaborate analysis. One might say that just as all nature presents itself to us as an extension of that which already exists, but, in each successive object in the rising scale, *with a difference;* so, knowledge of one thing after another is essentially an extension of that which is already known, to that which is like it, *but with a difference.* There is no break or leap.

Hence, if we are to instruct with effect, we always must build the new on the old, *i.e.* on what already is known.

*Principle of Method.* — LINK THE TEACHING OF THE NEW WITH FACTS ALREADY KNOWN WITH WHICH THE NEW HAS A REAL RELATION OF LIKENESS OR UNLIKENESS (*i.e.* LIKENESS IN UNLIKENESS), SO THAT THE GROWTH OF KNOWLEDGE MAY BE AN ORGANIC GROWTH.

RULES : —

(*a*) When introducing a new subject or a new lesson, go back upon what is already known.

(*b*) Prepare the mind for the lesson.

[I say likeness in unlikeness, for it seems to me that the association of contrast does not exist (a midge does not suggest an elephant), but that when carefully analysed it is likeness in unlikeness, or unlikeness in likeness, that really associates experiences.]

2. *Association as aiding Memory.* (Suggestion.)

The dynamical connection of experiences, which brings it about that one suggests the other to consciousness, is called the "Association of Ideas" (not a good name), and takes the following forms: —

### LAWS OR RULES OF ASSOCIATION.

(*a*)  *On the sensational plane* —

1. Contiguity in time or place (co-existent or in a series of sequence).
2. Likeness, and unlikeness in likeness.
3. The whole and the parts of a thing in a vague sensational way.

(*b*)  *On the plane of Will-reason.*

1. Whole and parts, viz. individual concepts and their elements or parts, suggest each other; general concepts and their parts suggest each other; reasonings, *i.e.* the three propositions of a syllogism, suggest each other.
2. Cause and effect suggest each other.

*Principle of Method.* — ASSOCIATE TEACHINGS SO AS TO AID MEMORY.

The growth of the fabric of mind, both in the dynamical sphere of sensation and in the self-conscious or purely active sphere of will, is always, as I have said above, through association of some kind. It is an organic growth. Hence the importance of the principle which we laid down, viz. Link teachings, so that the new shall grow out of the old (that which is already known). This cannot be done if we start a new subject or a new lesson without bringing into activity the existing material in the memory of the child, which is the natural basis for the next step. Psychologists treat Association too exclusively under its second and secondary head of Suggestion. The two aspects of Association taken together yield the following: —

*Principle of Method.* — ENRICH YOUR TEACHING WITH AS MANY RELEVANT ASSOCIATIONS AS POSSIBLE.[1]

## (4) MEMORY.

The first condition of memory, speaking generally, is the retention of what has once been present in consciousness.

It may be defined as the identifying a present consciousness with a consciousness formerly experienced.

1. *On the plane of sensation.*

Presentations and representations (images of presentations) are *felt* to be similar to prior presentations and representations. This we see in animals. *They* have, however, to wait for the action of their environment on them, or the dynamical movements in their cerebrum. This passivo-active memory may be called

*Reminiscence.*

2. *On the plane of reason.*

Here Will has entered, and the self-conscious subject seeks *purposely* to recover and reinstate past

---

[1] Education is an extensive as well as an intensive process.

experiences with a view to knowledge. This activo-active memory is to be called

*Recollection,*

and is, of course, peculiar to the man or rational mind alone.

It is manifest that in Reminiscence we are wholly in the hands of environment and Association, and that in Recollection we have to follow the track of Association in order to recover the past.

*Principle of Method.* — MEMORY SHOULD BE CULTI-VATED —

(a) As an act of Will, and therefore a discipline.

(b) As alone conserving the materials of knowledge.

(c) As an exercise facilitating the acquisition of new knowledge.

The conditions of remembering are —

> Vividness of impression (and accentuation by an act of Will);
>
> Duration of impression;
>
> Repetition of impression; but, above all,
>
> Association of the thing to be remembered with other things.

*Principle of Method.* — IN TEACHING REPEAT AND RE-REPEAT, REVISE AND RE-REVISE; AND BE ALWAYS FALLING BACK ON ELEMENTARY FACTS AND PRINCI-PLES RELATIVE TO THE SUBJECT OF INSTRUCTION, SO AS TO MAINTAIN THE SERIES OF ASSOCIATIONS.

*Note.* — The restrictions connected with the cultivation of memory, as such, demand consideration.

# PART III.

## *METHODOLOGY.*

# METHODOLOGY.

THE doctrine of Method is the last chapter in the theory or science of the education of a mind, and the first chapter of the Art or practice of education. It stands by itself, and consists simply of a gathering together of the principles which the discussion of mind as a *growing* or evolving organism has yielded. In so far as the theoretical argument is unsound, the principles of education deduced from it are unsound. This chapter, accordingly, merely brings together results already ascertained.

It is true that the human race, by the combined operation of inner tendency, self-evolved will, and pressure of environment, has somehow educated itself without the knowledge of these principles; also that successive generations of men have applied many of these principles in the form of empirical rules with more or less of mental confusion and more or less of success. The same remark, however, is applicable to political economy, political philosophy, and indeed to all science. None the less do we study the science of all subjects; and this both for the sake of knowledge in itself and for the improvement of practice. If we can by any possibility attain to a wise practice in the education of the human mind, we cannot doubt that it will be of vital importance to future generations of men.

### Summary of Principles.

The supreme End of the education of mind being ethical, that is to say, the expression of each *person* in self-directed daily conduct, we fairly enough deduce from this the principle —

1. TURN EVERYTHING TO USE.
   RULES : —
   (*a*) Teach nothing that is useless.
   (*b*) Connect all that is taught with the ordinary and everyday life of the pupil.
   (*c*) Call for the reproduction and application of what you teach. The ultimate test of exact knowledge is the power of applying it.
   (*d*) Turn what is known to use for yielding new knowledge.

2. FOLLOW THE ORDER OF MIND-GROWTH (which, speaking generally, is also the order of brain-growth).
   RULES : —
   (*a*) In teaching every subject, and every successive lesson on the same subject, build it up in the mind of the child in accordance with the order of mind-growth.
   (*b*) Proceed step by step, and step *after* step.

3. ENCOURAGE CONTACT WITH ALL FORMS OF EXISTENCE, AND PROMOTE ALL FORMS OF NATURAL ACTIVITY.

This, in order that there may be a rich substance of mind. (Education is an extensive as well as an intensive process.)

4. PRESENT TO SENSE.

RULE. — Never teach anything that can be seen, touched, heard, etc., without the presence of the object, or a vivid representation, of it;[1] and appeal to every sense, wherever practicable, in the teaching of every subject.

5. EVOKE THE WILL OF THE PUPIL.

*Note.* — Except in so far as a boy applies *himself* he knows nothing, but is a merely passivo-active creature of sensation. The child attains to knowledge, not by receiving it, but by *taking* it. He instructs himself. The teacher is the guide, co-operator, and remover of obstructions only.

This mode of teaching by throwing the work on the pupil gives him a pleasing sense of power and self-achievement which are in the highest degree stimulating.

6. TEACH ALL THAT IS COMPLEX ANALYTICO-SYNTHETICALLY, *i.e.* REDUCE AN OBJECT TO ITS ELEMENTS, AND THEN BUILD IT UP AGAIN.

7. PERCIPIENCE IS OF THE SINGLE, AND PERCEPTS LIE AT THE BASIS OF ALL KNOWLEDGE; THEREFORE,

---

[1] I should expect that magic lanterns would, ere long, be added to school apparatus.

TEACH ONE THING AT A TIME, WHETHER IT BE A
WHOLE OR AN ELEMENT IN A WHOLE.

RULES : —

(a) In object-lessons, etc., do not proceed to
the elements or properties of a thing
until the mind is accustomed to discriminate and name things as *wholes.*

(b) Dwell long over the simple elements of a
subject. Confusion in the beginning viti-
ates the whole after-process of learning.·

8. IN CONCIPIENCE PRACTISE PUPILS IN THE ANALY-
SIS OF COMPLEX THINGS AND THE SYNTHESIS OF MANY
PARTICULARS IN ONE WHOLE, IN ORDER TO TRAIN TO
EXACTNESS OF CONCEPTION (analytico-synthetic prin-
ciple).

*Note.* — This applies, first of all, to object-
lessons of every stage of difficulty up
to science instruction; but also to all
other subjects.

9. TEACH FIRST THE PROMINENT OR SALIENT CHAR-
ACTERISTICS OR ELEMENTS OF A THING (OR SUBJECT),
AND THEN PROCEED TO OTHER ELEMENTS.

RULE. — Confine yourself for a time to the
leading outlines of a subject, and then
fill in gradually (Geography, Grammar, History, etc.).

10. TEACH GENERALISATIONS AS GENERALISATIONS,
*i.e.* ADVANCE FROM THE PARTICULAR TO THE GENERAL,
FROM THE CONCRETE TO THE ABSTRACT.

*Note.* — When you encounter a generalisation
in the course of reading, analyse it

into its particulars, and put it together again (analytico-synthetic principle).

11. TEACH REASONINGS AS REASONINGS, *i.e.* GET
THE PUPIL TO MAKE EXPLICIT ALL IMPLICIT REASON-
INGS (analytico-synthetic principle).

12. COMPLETE YOUR INSTRUCTION IN A SUBJECT BY
TEACHING THROUGH CAUSES (analytico-synthetic principle).

13. PRESENT A GOOD MODEL OF WHAT YOU WISH
THE PUPIL TO DO (Writing, Drawing, Carpentering,
Composition, etc.).

Grown men are imitative, but children most of
all; they do what they see *you* do.

14. CULTIVATE THE IMAGINATION.

15. ASSOCIATE TEACHINGS, *i.e.* ALWAYS LINK THE
NEW WITH WHAT IS ALREADY KNOWN. THIS IS ESSEN-
TIAL TO THE ORGANIC GROWTH OF KNOWLEDGE AND
TO INTELLECTUAL INTEREST; AND, CONSEQUENTLY, TO
SUCCESSFUL TEACHING.

RULE. — *Prepare the mind of the pupil for a*
*lesson, so that there may be no abrupt*
*transition.* The mind does not take
leaps.

16. ASSOCIATE TEACHINGS IN ORDER TO AID THE
MEMORY.

The Association should be a *real* association; but
failing this the external associations of contiguity in time and place may be taken advantage of.

17. AS TO ASSOCIATION GENERALLY.

RULES: —

(a) Support and enrich your teaching of a subject with as many illustrative and *relevant* associations as possible. (This not only helps the memory, but gives breadth and pliancy to mind.)

(b) Let all associations with your teaching be pleasing, so that there may be no physical or moral obstruction to the natural growth of knowledge.

18. CULTIVATE THE MEMORY.

RULE. — Repeat and re-repeat, revise and re-revise, always falling back on the elementary facts and principles of the subject taught. Thus the memory of a subject is the memory of real relations, and not of mere words and formulæ, which is *rote* instruction or cram. *Repetitio mater Studiorum.*

Our survey of elementary physiology taught us the great fact of physiological *habit* and its relation to all intellectual and moral activity. All functions of mind, intellectual and ethical, are strengthened and made easy by use.

19. THEREFORE, REPEAT AND RE-REPEAT THE SAME INTELLECTUAL OPERATIONS IN CONNECTION WITH A CONTINUOUS SUBJECT, WITH A VIEW TO THE FORMATION OF A GOOD INTELLECTUAL HABIT.

This alone is true training and discipline, for this alone is permanent in its effects.

" Use almost can change the stamp of nature."
*Hamlet,* iii. 4.

The above scheme of Method is a summarised statement of the Art of education, in so far as intelligence is concerned, and it is applicable to all possible subjects of instruction (including the ethical, as we shall see).

To instruct well is to instruct (consciously or unconsciously) in accordance with these principles and rules, *i.e.* in accordance with Method. It is necessary to instruct according to Method, if our instruction is to be sound and sure, and, above all, if we are to train and discipline (*i.e.* educate) mind. And this is the point to emphasise, that training and discipline is greater than knowledge, and that *only by sound method* can we train and discipline faculty. Method derives its chief importance from this.[1]

The point chiefly to note in connection with these rules of the Art is that they are ascertained, not empirically (though many of them had been found out long before psychology was applied to education), but scientifically. That is to say, they flow by necessary deduction from the science of Mind.

Thus it is that we vindicate for the *art* of education

---

[1] Strange that classical teachers, who are most of all identified with the theory that discipline is all in all, have been most active in the defence of " No method."

a prior and governing *science.*   Take any of these rules you choose, and go back on our statement of the processes of intelligence, and you will see for yourselves its scientific basis.   If we can ascertain (as we can) *how* it is that mind knows and grows, *how* it is that intelligence intelligises, it is clear as noonday that we have also got the *how* of teaching, because teaching is simply helping the mind to perform its function of knowing and growing.

These principles and rules, I would repeat, as the issue of scientific analysis, form the last chapter of the Science of education, and at the same time the first chapter of the Art.   All the subsequent chapters of the Art are merely the application of this chapter to the various subjects which we wish boys and girls to learn.   We have nothing to add to them except this, that their practical application from day to day is modified by two considerations, viz., *First,* the circumstances (by which I mean mental rather than physical circumstances) of the pupil.   *Secondly,* the subject we are teaching.   Not that the principles do not apply to all subjects, but that each subject will suggest its own expedients, if not also rules.

I shall explain these two points: —

As regards the first: if the pupils to whom I am giving object-lessons or any other lessons are of the more educated classes of society, it is absurd to make oneself a slave to the rule of "little by little" and "step by step" to the extent to which we subject ourselves to it when dealing with poor children whose minds receive no home cultivation.   In the case of the former, we can take much for granted and advance more rapidly than with the latter. This consideration is of greater weight in some subjects than in others, *e.g.* in examining on the reading-lesson. You can yourselves, after a little reflection, supply all that I omit saying in this connection. The age of the pupils, too, is one of the most important of the conditions under which we teach. Setting aside the question of the age at which a natural science can be taught *scientifically,* all will at once see that with boys of fourteen we must proceed much more slowly than with boys of sixteen or seventeen. The lecture on the periods or stages of mental growth will suggest to the thoughtful reader all that has to be said on the question of rapidity of progress.

As regards the second point: — additions to the rules, or modifications of them, are naturally suggested to anybody's common sense by the nature of the subject he happens to be teaching. For example, the mode of procedure in teaching the English language is fundamentally the same as that to be followed in teaching French or Latin. But the fact that English is the native tongue admits of a procedure which is impossible in the case of a foreign tongue. The most important difference of procedure is suggested by the fact that English grammar is, in the mind of the child, implicit. We are merely making explicit, and reducing to order and rule, what is already there. It is plain that we cannot do this in the case of French or Latin. On the other hand, presuming that all will agree with me in thinking that the native grammar must be the basis of foreign grammars (in order that the new may grow out of the old and knowledge be an organic growth), then it is absurd not to take advantage of English grammar in teaching French or Latin, and not to assume that a good deal of the grammatical work is already done to my hand. And so on, as when we pass from Latin to Greek. Here common sense comes in; and though it be "the rarest gift of Heaven," we must take it for certain that all teachers are endowed with it.

And this allusion to common sense suggests that I must still make one remark before I conclude this part of my subject.

It is possible to overdo method.

You may be giving a lesson quite in accordance with sound method, but you may be pedantically taking step after step with too exclusive an eye on method of procedure, and too little regard to the subject you are teaching, the mental condition of the pupil you are teaching, and the proposed end of your teaching. You may forget entirely that the prime condition of all successful method is the sympathetic movement of the mind before you with your mind, and your mind with his. Indeed, without this sympathy, subtle and delicate in its nature, your method becomes wooden and lifeless. This, now, is to be a slave to method, whereas method ought to be your servant, not your master. Sympathy cannot be taught by any professor of education. It is a thing of native growth, but its germs may be cultivated. The greatest stimulus to a young mind, you may be sure, is your sympathy with it, for this is always accompanied with a genuine desire to lead the pupil into the subject; and that desire will in all, save a few cases, be reciprocated by the pupil. There is no device for commanding attention and no methodology which can be a substitute for interest in your subject and sympathy with the mind before you. In fact, one might almost supersede all study of method if one could only secure this, that the teacher was able sympathetically to place himself in the mental attitude of the pupil towards the lesson, and advance along with him step by step to the full comprehension of it.

It has also, I think, to be noted that it is above all *that* philosophy of mind which regards mind as being, under more or less disguise, a process of sense-agglutination, which will generate a method in the forming of mind as pedantic in practice as it is unsound in theory. The growth of a mind, even if we regard it as a mere fabric of stones and cement, is not dependent on the educator. It fulfils its own life in its own way. We merely fix the end, give direction, supply defects, remove obstructions, and, generally, lend a hand. Some would build up mind as if they were laying a tessellated pavement. Method which does not confine itself to the order of studies and the discipline and development of faculty generally, but condescends to the minutest details of the order of questions to be put even in a simple narrative lesson, is method run to seed. The human mind, as a living energy, is always arranging its own material for itself, and children are not so dull as some method-mongers seem to imagine. Still more clearly shall we see the fallacy of the pedantic extremist in method, if we recognise reason as at root a will-energy ever seeking, by the necessity of its own nature, to correlate presentations and representations under the stimulus of the native form of End. To stimulate and direct this, taking care to keep to the highway of mind-process, is more than half our task.

In short, one great advantage accruing to the study of the science of education, as distinguished from the art as a dogmatic system, is, that it makes the student-teacher master of method, and prevents method, in the sense of rules, being master of him. He sees the ultimate ground and significance of the rules, and feels free and unencumbered in his use of them. His obedience is the obedience of a freeman, not of a slave. He is the subject of a constitutional monarch, not of a despot. We rightly despise " rule of thumb "; but let us remember that there is such a thing as a pedantic system of rules which becomes a kind of organised " rule of thumb " — perhaps a more dangerous enemy of true method than the traditionary practices which make no pretensions.

*Note.* — There ought to follow Methodology, a discussion of the art of examining and a consideration of *manner* in the teacher as distinguished from method. On these subjects much might be said. As to the art of examining, I would say generally, that the moment it departs from the type of an intelligent conversation conducted with perfect naturalness, it goes wrong.

# PART IV.

*APPLIED METHODOLOGY, OR THE ART OF EDUCATION.*

# APPLIED METHODOLOGY, OR THE ART OF EDUCATION.

METHOD OF INTELLECTUAL EDUCATION, *i.e.* OF INSTRUCTION AND DISCIPLINE.[1]

I DO not say methods of instruction, but of "intellectual *education*," because it has been already shown that all sound instruction of the intelligence involves training and discipline, and all sound training and discipline of the intelligence can be secured through sound instruction alone. The two taken together constitute the education of mind as intelligence.

We divided subjects of instruction into two classes, the *Real*, which specially feed the mind, and the *Formal* or *Abstract*, which specially discipline. The Real comprised Naturalistic and Humanistic subjects; and so with the Formal. We shall take the Real first.[2]

---

[1] The practical application of Method to the various subjects of instruction would naturally extend to about twenty-five lectures.

[2] There is also, doubtless, a *reality* of fact and relation in the abstract.

195

A. — *Application of Method to Instruction in the* REAL.

*The Naturalistic.* — (1) Object-lessons and Nature-knowledge.   Elementary service generally.

(2) Knowledge of the Human Body.

(3) Geography (as defined in Lecture V., Part I.).[1]

(4) Physiography.

*The Humanistic.*

*Introductory.* — Reading as a merely instrumental art.   Writing as a subsidiary instrument.

(1) Language,[2] *i.e.* —

(*a*) The Vernacular language as the expression of the thought of others — Literature.

(*b*) The Vernacular language as a synthetic exercise — the expression of one's own thought — Imitative Composition.

(2) Foreign Languages as Literature.

(3) Economics.

(4) History with Civil Relations.

(5) Moral Sentiments and Precepts [Minor Morals].

---

[1] For a paper on "Method in Teaching Geography," see *Occasional Addresses.*

[2] The substance of my lectures on Language and Literature will be found in the book entitled *Language and Linguistic Method in the School* (Cambridge University Press).   The student is also referred to "Theory and the Curriculum of the Secondary School," in *Teachers' Guild Addresses* (Percival & Co.), and to "Liberal Education in the Primary School," in *Occasional Addresses* (Cambridge University Press).

(6) Spiritual Ideas (including the Beautiful) and Religion.

B.—*Application of Method to Instruction in the* FORMAL.

Drawing.
Arithmetic.
Geometry.

Language as Grammar (native and foreign languages).
Rhetoric.
Logic.

The lecturer on education will treat all the above subjects in detail. I merely name them here.

*Note.* — The inclusion of drawing among " Formal " subjects may give rise to question. I regard outline drawing (including geometrical) as belonging to the formal of *sense,* and as an essential element in all education of the intelligence. Apart from numerous other advantages, the practice of drawing must tend to give a definiteness of outline to all mental operations: these have a tendency to visualisation as they become absolutely clear and distinct. The *effort* also to copy a line or curve so that it shall be a true copy, is an effort of self-directed will which is of disciplinary benefit, and yet within the capacity of the youngest.

As to materials of education generally, I would here lay down two propositions which ought to be constantly present to the teacher as governing all that can be said as to " materials."

I. The child of six or seven may, without exaggeration, be said to come to school from the home, the fields, and the streets with his mind full of the elements of *every department of knowledge* included in the above classification. He is already a walking miniature encyclopædia. We are much mistaken if we think his mind is waiting for us before it begins to work. It is chockful of judgments. The subjects included above under the heads Real and Formal are (with

the exception of foreign tongues), if closely examined, merely
a generalisation and classification of the materials in and
through which the life of each is being carried on as a
matter of course.

II. The teacher's main business is to take the chaotic
child-synthesis to pieces, make clear what is confused, and
build on the foundations thus laid. But the teacher never
leaves behind him the ordinary experiences of child-life; he
simply interprets and extends them. It is daily life which
gives material, and the school which gives interpretation,
direction, and form. Life and the school should be in a
continual reciprocity — never disjoined. *Vitæ non scholæ
discendum est.*

---

We have now come to the end of that portion of
the Institutes of Education which deals with RIGHT
JUDGMENT, including as elements of right judgment,
and therefore as materials of instruction, moral and
spiritual ideas. But knowledge, and even wisdom,
which issue in judging knowingly and wisely, are of
little avail, save in so far as they express themselves
in "Good action under a sense of Duty," and find their
completion in a "comprehension of the spiritual significance of nature and life" (p. 33). Thus alone do
we achieve the Ethical End; and we must now indicate the lines and method of instruction, training, and
discipline in respect of this the ultimate aim of all
our endeavours.

# PART V.

*ETHICAL EDUCATION — SPECIALLY
CONSIDERED.*

# LECTURE I.

ETHICAL IDEAS AS THE REAL, OR SUBSTANCE, OF LIFE.

NOTE. — *The following lectures consist of summaries and paragraphs only. It is presumed that the student now turns back and re-peruses Lectures IV. and V. Part I.*

THE problem of education may be summarised, as we have seen, under the three heads of the end, the means (which comprehends materials and process), and the agency, which sets the whole in motion and carries it out to its completion. The agency is the teacher, who passes into the higher category of "educator" only when he works under the inspiration of an ethical purpose. On his personality so much depends that the determination of ends and the discussion of materials and processes seem to sink into comparative insignificance. But were we to consider this personality itself (which lies outside our plan in this book), we should find that in the teacher, as in education generally, it is the ethical which is of supreme moment. No system of training can guarantee ethical fitness; but it can shape to an excellent issue the ethical predisposition, and constrain those endowed by nature with this predisposition seriously to ponder the best ways of fulfilling their obligations to their own educational ideal and to the national life.

The teacher who is ethically endowed will see that the materials which he uses for knowledge, and the discipline which he gives by means of these materials have for their ultimate object the fitting of the young to interpret their daily experience, subduing all to the service of an ethical ideal. But knowledge and intellectual discipline alone, he is well aware, even when animated by an ethical purpose, will not of themselves suffice; instruction must be given in ethical ideas themselves as the true and ultimate realities of life, and direct discipline must also be given in ethical habit.

We find, as the last result of human experience, certain moral ideas ready made for us. This is ethical tradition. Ethical Education consists in training the young so as to put them in possession of these ideas as motives of conduct, and as necessary to their ethical completeness. Thus we build up Conscience in them. Left to his own individual experience, a man's knowledge would be small, his conception of human relations restricted, and his interpretation of them false or inadequate.

The moral "ideas" are high generalisations, and (as we now know) we can introduce children effectively to generalisations only through the particulars of conduct. We build up the idea through particular thoughts and acts. Children are our modern instances of primitive man. Their minds have to repeat the mental history of the past, in their conceptions of duty as well as in their knowledge of things.

How do we proceed with a view to put them in possession of their inheritance?

*First,* We take care to instruct them in so much of the accumulated materials of knowledge — knowledge of things — as will enable them to form right judgments, and give fulness to life by multiplying interests. The subjects we select and the method of giving instruction in them, with a view to the attainment of our ultimate ethical purpose, constitute that part of educational theory and method which has to do with the intellect primarily; that is to say, the mere understanding of things and their relations. All this we have considered in the previous lectures; and as we enter on the specific consideration of the ethical, we see that a liberal and generous course of instruction is necessary, if the circle of thought and interests is to be so widened as to give materials for sound ethical conclusions. The width, no less than the intensity, of a man's intellectual and ethical life is the measure of his education.

*Secondly,* We *regulate the conduct* of the young in accordance with moral ideas and the sentiment of duty.

*Thirdly,* We *instruct* them in moral ideas themselves, and their spiritual significance.

Our object in these processes is one and the same — to produce in each human being an ethical state of mind; but this again with a view to expression and action, which alone give value to the ethical *state:* in other words, we aim at producing a certain state of being, and *effective virtue* as sole guarantee of the reality of that state.

Now as to the third step, it has to be noted generally that no one can get a *knowledge* of moral or spiritual ideas by merely acquiescing in propositions regarding them. All moral ideas which can constitute motives of action arise primarily out of feelings — "inner sense," and, consequently, we get possession of them only by *feeling* them — feeling, and *so* seeing, their truth, and the *law* that is inherent in them. In the same way we do not get a knowledge of anything of external sense by reading statements about it, but only by feeling it, that is to say, having it present to the senses. There is this difference, however, between the intellectual and the ethical, that knowledge of subjects completes itself simply as knowledge (although until we can *use* it, it is not wholly ours), whereas ethical ideas do not truly live at all, save in action. We never, consequently, can be said even to know them (feel them), until we have carried them into action; or, at least, realised them imaginatively, if not in our own activity, then in the activity of another.

# LECTURE II.

WHEN dealing with the philosophy of mind as an intellectual or reason-activity, we first exhibited the characteristics of the sensational intelligence of the animal; and we thus gained a clearer comprehension of the distinctive characteristics of the intelligence of man, who alone is a reason. The same mode of procedure will be followed now in the ethical sphere.

### Animal and Infant Ethics.

The result of our analysis (p. 73) was that the simple feelings which are inherent in a fully developed animal organism are the following: —

1. The Feeling of *Life*-activity.
2. The natural appetites (impulses, instincts) working from within.
3. Sympathy of being and of natural feelings in living creatures.
4. The feeling of kindness to other living creatures, especially among those of a like kind (goodwill).
5. The feeling of pleasure in kindness received from others (love of approbation).

6. The feeling of a superior power (with the consequent feeling of dependence).
7. The feeling of resistance to anything which may hurt (animal courage).
8. The feeling of fear, or of evasion, of anything which may hurt (animal cowardice).
9. The feeling of rivalry.

All these insist on manifesting themselves as occasion arises.

Man shares all these feelings, as instincts, desires, impulses, with animals; and they form the basis of his ethical nature. As basis of his nature, they are in evidence from the first; indeed they constitute the whole ethical apparatus of the infant. There is no harm in them; but, on the contrary, good: and the young must be allowed to pursue their desires and exercise their activities in every direction. We gradually mould these to law, but we must not be in too great haste.

In man, reason (as Will) enters for the purpose of rationalising all these impulses and directing them to ends, which ends are, in their ultimate form, ethical ideas; and these, taken together, constitute the ideal of conduct for each man.

The business of the teacher and parent is to train and discipline this Will and to build up this Ideal.

The animal is a mere victim of the dynamic of feeling. It yields to that which is strongest or uppermost at the moment. Man, on the contrary, directs feeling and emotion in certain special lines of activity, *i.e.* towards certain specific ends, by virtue of the reason in him. These ends are, as I have said, ethical ideas, and they constitute motives of action as generalised.

Further, when this Will-reason enters into the sphere of feeling, it brings with it new material to Consciousness — (1) A consciousness of Will as a determining power, energy, or force. (2) A consciousness of personality or self. (3) A consciousness of duty to moral law as inherent in the ideas and the ideal constituted by Will-reason.

With education these rational elements of man's distinctive ethical nature grow in strength.

The sum of the ethical ideas of conduct in a man, taken along with the perception of law in these ideas, and of consequent duty to that law as supreme, constitute, taken together, what we call *Conscience*. The function of the educator, accordingly, may be said to be to build up Conscience in the young: and Conscience, I repeat, may be succinctly defined as the ideal system of motives, along with the sentiment of law and duty to law as inherent in that ideal system.

As to these Ideas themselves: they are ascertained thus: Reason dealing with the feelings and emotions which we have in common with animals (though in more ample measure) determines the relations of a person to himself and to other persons, and so constitutes the moral ideas (ends and motives). These ideas are all complex.

The most common of them are —

| | |
|---|---|
| Humanity (which is good-will to others, and love of goodwill of others). | Courage. |
| | Integrity. |
| Justice. | Resoluteness and Perseverance. |
| Truthfulness. | Purity. |
| Honesty. | Reverence (for that which |
| Honour. | is greater than our- |
| Fidelity. | selves). |

Self-control *and* Self-respect or self-worth.

The analysis of these complex ideas into their elements of emotion and reason must throw light on the method of educating the young, so that the ideas shall be to them a permanent possession as knowledge.

I do not attempt this analysis here, but content myself with saying that the teacher should always have present to himself, as dominating aim, the cultivation in the pupil of self-control and self-respect, and of those more generic and supreme ethical ideas which comprehend others, viz. the idea of HUMANITY, which expands and enriches the soul, while at the same time determining conduct, and the spiritual idea of GOD as universal Father, which at once humbles and exalts the personality, and Whose best service is the service of mankind. The pupil should early know that a continuous struggle is appointed for man, not only with his animal nature and material interests, but with the very self-conscious ego, which, just because it lifts him above nature, is too apt to rest content with self-worship.

I have spoken elsewhere, in detail, of specific Religious teaching.[1] Accordingly, I would confine myself here to saying that where there is a breach between ethical and religious teaching, we have neither the one nor the other in its fulness of significance. Without religious teaching, the education of a human being is (on purely psychological grounds) demonstrably incomplete.

*Law and Duty.* — I have referred to Law and Duty as *residing in the ideas.* We may put it otherwise thus: the abstract sentiment of law and duty inherent in the reason of man is a mere empty Form, and has to be filled with the substance of real or ethical ideas which are to regulate life and conduct. This sentiment of law, implying reverence for, and duty to, law, accompanies all our training and instruction, and is taken for granted as an ever-present inner fact distinguishing the man-child from the animal. Through this sentiment of law and duty, in truth, we must mainly work, although we do not always make our procedure apparent to the child.

The educator may be assured that the child is ever in search of law. Were there no ideal and law for man there could be no morality; one act would be as good as another.

The discipline of duty to law is essentially a calling forth of *effort* to will the good and right in the face of difficulties.

---

[1] *Occasional Addresses* and *Teachers' Guild Addresses.*

In this connection, again, the recognition of God as
source of law, and of the world as a moral order, is to
be continually fostered (by being assumed rather than
inculcated), until it reaches that clearness of vision,
possible only to the maturing or matured mind, which
contemplates God as not only the true and ever-
abiding *life* of the spirit of man, but the ever-during
*law* of that spirit.

# LECTURE III.

UNITY OF THE INTELLECTUAL AND ETHICAL IN
EDUCATION.

*Nutrition and Discipline: Real and Formal.*

WILL in so far as, in its reason-process, it affirms
or posits real ethical ends or ideas as also *abstract law,*
is, as we now may see, the Formal element in ethics.
In other words, Will, engaging itself with abstract
duty to law, and acting for the sake of duty to law as
such, is *Formal.* The ethical ideal, on the other hand,
which is "constituted law" for us, is the substance or
matter, in other words, the *Real* in the ethical act.

We have spoken in past pages [1] of the unity of
reason; but we now farther see that the human mind
as a whole is a rational unity. There is no true
separation of the intellectual and the ethical. The
ethical is within the sphere of the rational, not outside
it or somehow added on to.it. The rational affirmation of end in the sphere of inner feeling and emotion,
which affirmation determines conduct, is identical in
its nature with rational affirmation regarding anything
whatsoever.

---

[1] *Vide* also Appendix D.

211

*Note.* — Within the limits of mere knowledge, the affirmation has its final issue in knowledge simply; the moment it goes beyond this, and involves the effecting of a particular knowledge in the world of action or conduct, the knowledge, it will be found, is, *ipso facto*, instinct with some feeling or emotion, and becomes ethical. The abstract love of pure knowledge itself, for its own sake, is, however, ethical, because it is the pursuit of an idea and an ideal. This involves emotion.

In the purely intellectual sphere we distinguished between the Real and the Formal or Abstract in instruction. So, in the distinctively Ethical sphere — the ethical side of reason — there is a Real and a Formal or Abstract.

Accordingly, just as we found Will in the conscious subject to be root and nerve of reason in man, we now find the same Will to be root and nerve of all ethical life and activity. The ethical end, — always an idea of reason, — which is affirmed as right and law, is carried, by the sustained energy of the same Will that affirmed it, into action; and thus we become ethical beings, and not knowing beings only.

It will be at once seen that this analysis of the essential nature of mind not only gives to us, as students of philosophy, a unity of view, but as students of education a unity of theory and system. For in the education of both the rational and ethical nature, Will is the distinguishing characteristic of man — that whereby he is man; and it is this, consequently, that we have specially to train. and discipline, viz. Will as at once a rational and an ethical energy.

But, inasmuch as rational mind, as pure Will and its Reason-process (or, as I prefer to call it, Will-reason), is merely formal, we have to provide food, reality, nutrition for the moral, just as we do for the intellectual, nature. This material is, we now know, ethical ideas. We must never, however, lose sight of the fact that it is the command which Will has over its materials, and the ends for which it uses them, that are alone of value in life. A purpose of Duty is demanded of us. This, indeed, is what we mean when we say that the end of education, as of life, is ethical.

Intellectual *discipline*, we found, involves a self-initiated energy of Will in the face of difficulties under a sense of Law — that is to say, the fulfilment of law as imposed by another or oneself with a view to the fulfilment of a purpose: Ethical *discipline* also may be defined in the same terms. Thus, intellectual discipline is, in truth, a moral discipline.

The above remarks justify the traditionary attitude of the classical humanists to *discipline* of intellect as of supreme importance; but it also shows that they have erred in making it all-important. The intellect must be fed, and the ethical nature must be fed. So essential is this, that we might also justify the realistic attitude of mind to education as of supreme importance.

The true conclusion is that to which we formerly came. Will-reason can be trained and disciplined only in and through the Real: and the Real can be effectively taught only when it is so taught as to be a training and discipline of the Formal in mind. How? To this scientific methodology is the answer; and as regards intellect we have nothing more to say. But methodology is equally potent in the ethical sphere.

# PART VI.

*APPLIED METHODOLOGY AS ART OF ETHICAL EDUCATION.*

# LECTURE I.

*Instruction, Training, and Discipline generally.*

ETHICAL Education, I have just said, comprises (like intellectual education) two elements, the *Real* and the *Formal* — nutrition and training with discipline.

I pointed out (p. 41) the distinction between the "training" and "discipline" of the intelligence. Discipline, we found, could not be distinguished from training except in this, that it was dependent on spontaneous, unaided, and self-directed effort on the part of the pupil, with a view to the effecting of a self-conscious purpose; while training was the carrying of the pupil through certain intellectual processes by a stronger will — his master's. Hence we found that formal or abstract studies were in themselves more disciplinary, if rightly taught, than realistic studies, because they involved greater initial energy and more sustained application of that Will which, as a power and process, is the distinguishing differentia of man. The same distinction is apparent in ethical education. In the case of very young children we *train* to right action, *i.e.* we guide, lead, and help them to do the

217

right, in obedience to their teacher as a moral instructor: we do not appeal to abstract law, or lay a
burden on their wills.    We rely on imitation and on
their affection for us.    As they grow older, however,
we *call* upon them to do the right of themselves in the
face of temptation, in obedience to the moral law in
them, and as an act of self-directing will in the service
of bare duty: this is formal discipline.

Thus far, the method of intellectual and the method
of moral education run on parallel lines.    In both
alike training is the guidance and helping of the
unformed will in the fulfilment of ends, and discipline
is the spontaneous, free energising of that will in the
fulfilment of self-conscious ends, to which, as law, it
owes Duty.

# LECTURE II.

THE ethical differs from the intellectual as regards
the method of *instruction* only in so far as we are now
instructing in the emotions and ideas which constitute
the inner substance or matter of our ethical life. The
difference is caused by this: in the sphere of intellectual education we have to do with presentation and
acquisition, whereas in the sphere of ethical education
·we have directly to do with action or conduct; for, as
we pointed out, an emotion is not ours till it is felt,
and an ethical idea is not truly ours till it is used.
An ethical emotion or idea truly lives only in action,
and, accordingly, can be realised as a fact of consciousness by the child, and so truly *known*, only as an act.

The distinction is, fundamentally, the distinction
between outer sense and inner feeling respectively as
yielding materials for knowledge.

Consequently, we *instruct in the real of ethics chiefly
by training.*

That is to say, (a) we do not bring the ethical before
the child's mind as a series of perceptive facts or
reasoned conclusions, but let the child contemplate
ethical emotions and ideas in action in ourselves or in

others (either actually or in narratives). Perception is here perception of a *feeling* in activity. (*b*) Above all, we lead him to imitate and do the good instead of the bad by letting him *feel* its inherent attractiveness, which he does instinctively; and, further, by associating the good with his regard for us.

Hence it is, that while the principle of method — "present a good model" — is of general application in the instruction of the intelligence, it is absolutely indispensable in ethical instruction. In fact, it may be said that abstract instruction in emotions or in moral ideas or precepts is to the young nothing but words — *verba sine rebus.* The *res* in this sphere are actions resting on emotions and ideals. The process of acquisition is the imitative adoption of what the child approves in others, especially his Teacher. Only then does he truly *know* the ethical emotion. So with himself; he must *do* that he may *know.* Logically, it is true, the virtuous state of *being* must always precede "effective virtue"; but, as a matter of fact, the two are so indissolubly united in the life of mind, that we would seem to bring about the virtuous state of being by first securing in the young the *doing* of the right; and so we work backwards.

These remarks apply also to specifically religious instruction. I build up the reverential frame of mind, for example, by means of the habitual *act* of prayer and the exhibition in my own conduct of a consciousness of the Divine presence. This is sympathetically adopted by the child, and he *knows* it in the moment of *doing* it and seeing me do it.

The feelings, again, which lie at the root of minor morals (which Locke calls good breeding) are all taught by imitation and a training in acts. Far too little importance, I would here point out, is attached by teachers to minor morals in their reactive influence on character in its deeper sense. No verbal instruction is here of much avail. Good breeding, acquired after a youth is grown up, is always alien to him. His manners and "form" are self-conscious. He is wearing somebody else's clothes, and they never quite fit.

The general conclusion is that ethical *instruction*, is through *training*, *i.e.* by evoking in the child the sympathetic approval and imitation of good acts. Coercion would defeat our purpose. The child has to adopt our point of view through imitation, and imitation rests, as we have seen, psychologically on sympathy: how can there be sympathy with that which a child fears? It would be a contradiction in terms.

At the same time, I do not admit that cold precept is always out of place with the young. It sums up the character of actions, and has a function in the sphere of the emotions similar to formulated statements in the sphere of knowledge. Still less is it to be held that the poetic or other eloquent expression of moral sentiment is ever out of place. On the contrary, so long as a poem or rhetorical prose expresses ethical sentiments or ideas which are fairly well understood, they are powerful agents in building up the ethical ideal at every stage of education; especially when, as in the case of poetry, the words are allied with music

in the school.   For, all that has to do with the expression of the ideal, in words or in beautiful forms, is
moralising, simply because it is ideal.

Precepts and dogmas, however, are generalisations,
and no generalisation, as I have so often said, has any
meaning except in so far as it sums up particular
experiences.   In the intellectual sphere, particular
experiences are percepts and concepts (individual) of
*things;* in the ethical sphere they are the *acts* of the
learner himself, or of his teacher and companions, or
the imaginative realising of the acts of others as
narrated in prose or poetry.

If this distinction be clearly understood, it will be
found that, as regards all else, ethical instruction is
subject to the same Principles of method as intellectual instruction, and we do not require to start in
search of a specific ethical methodology.   To show this
in detail would encumber this book, but the mere quoting of a few of the Principles will show what I mean.

*Present to Sense:*—that is to say, evoke the moral
feeling or emotion so that it shall be clearly present
to consciousness.   No preaching will do this any more
than preaching about a banana will convey to consciousness the sense-concept of a banana.   Emotions,
etc., must be presented to inner sense as *acts*.

*Present a good model.*

*Evoke the Will.*

*Turn to Use: i.e.* Help the child in his daily acts to
put into practice what he has seen and approved in
your acts and the acts of others.   Without supervision,
moral training is impossible; but the supervision
should be sympathetic and easy.

*Let the instruction be analytico-synthetic:* that is to say, in historical and biographical readings, and in poetical reading, the complex of conduct exhibited has to be analysed, and its elements, moral and immoral, to be brought into light with a view to a correct synthesis of the whole. Only so is the lesson of any use at all. But do not overdo this. If you are to produce a flame easily with Bryant & May's matches, attend to the direction on the box, " Rub lightly."

*Associate ethical teachings :* — that is to say, not only so as to exhibit their unity in Will, etc., but associate them also with pleasant surroundings; above all, a pleasant countenance.

The other principles and rules of Method I leave you to apply for yourselves.

But in leaving this subject I cannot forego one remark suggested by the master principle, " Evoke the Will." The child must do the work of his *own* moral education under your guidance simply, just as he does the work of instruction under your guidance. Do not emphasise and drive home moral teachings too much as if the child were an *unwilling* recipient of them. Assume that the young mind is ready for them, nay, eager for them; and while you handle moral and spiritual things gravely, let all austerity be absent.

# LECTURE III.

By the formal or abstract in ethics we mean Law, and Duty to Law as such; and here the principles "Evoke the Will" and "Turn to Use" are specially applicable.

The ethical ideas which constitute the real or substance of morality cannot be trusted to determine a man's conduct, still less a boy's, save in ordinary cases. Outside the ordinary and usual, the sense of duty to abstract Law, and *that* as Law of God, is indispensable.

It is the *Law* in ethical ideas, consequently, and obedience to that Law, which we must constantly keep before the young if we are to educate them so as to give them power over their own actions — capacity for free self-regulation as they grow in years. This evoking of moral energy in the face of difficulties, is what is meant by moral discipline. Our aim is a "Habit of good action under a sense of Duty."

Will, as reason, *knows* and realises in consciousness the ethical idea; and it is the same Will which realises the knowledge in action. The continued suprem-

224

acy of this Will, as serving moral *Law*, is the Habit of Virtue.

But the child knows nothing of inner Law, and the boy knows little. It is abstract, and in germ only as yet. The young are concrete beings of sense and feeling. The educator (parent, teacher, the state) is to them Law — Law in its concrete and visible form. This is their Conscience, as yet external to them, and preceding, evoking, and guiding the natural growth of inner Law in them.

For the securing of the habitual recognition of Law as Law, and as an end in itself for the free energy of Will (the essential characteristic of man as a good citizen and as a person), a great deal depends on the behaviour of this *external* Conscience — viz. Authority or Law as embodied in the parent, the state, and the teacher. The method of Moral Discipline, then, is through Authority.

It might be asked at this point, What Right has a schoolmaster thus to impose himself, as Law, on the young ? The answer is, The right of the mature mind to direct the immature mind, the right conferred by a man's being the holder of the tradition of Law which is accumulated wisdom, and the right inherent in the parent and the State, — all which are embodied in the Teacher for the time being.

This is his Right. Right may ultimately have to be supported by Might. But Might, in so far as it is not used in the service of Right, has no right, and is immoral; consequently, ineffective and demoralising. Nay, even in the service of Right, it is ineffective and demoralising when employed without absolute necessity. For Might as such (mere physical force) can never moralise. Through sympathy alone the child imitatively adopts the Law in you and from you. Doubtless, Might can deter from certain external acts and protect law-abiding citizens from their internal enemies; and, consequently, in a State it is indispensable as a protective police. In the school, too, Might can deter; but inasmuch as the purpose of the school is education, it is an ethical purpose — the attainment of certain *positive* ethical results in the pupils of self-directing wills — and the merely deterrent, consequently, cannot educate. In truth, we might almost go so far as to say that, except in so far as the young acquiesce in the law of their elders, the effect of law is demoralising. You cannot form character outside the will of the child. It is a miserable result of education, which can be identified with the merely negative result of a State police.

We conclude that the Authority which demands and commands obedience to Law, in the family and school, is MORAL AUTHORITY, not Coercive Might. The whole subject of Discipline to Law and Duty, then, centres round this question of moral authority.

# LECTURE IV.

THE immature mind is not capable of apprehending the conception of abstract Law and Duty, as I have already said. This conception is there in germ and becomes explicit gradually through the discipline of young minds, which by nature are seeking for Law and going out to meet it. Discipline, it might be said, is attained when we have formed the habit of obedience to the *external* Law — the Moral Authority of the teacher. Not so: the habit must be *so* formed as to be a habit of free obedience to inner Law, and a perpetual recognition of its majesty. It is a slow process, and the teacher must pursue his aim deliberately, calmly, and persistently. If the young were capable of realising the abstract conception of formal law, we should content ourselves with saying that sympathy with the teacher and imitation of him and of other good examples would suffice, as is the case of instruction. But they are not capable. The abstract has here, as everywhere, to be learned through the concrete. The teacher is the concrete. Now, since the teacher embodies moral authority for the purpose of regulating the acts of the pupil and so disciplining him in

227

duty to law, he himself must make sure that he *is a true and worthy moral authority.* So far as he is this, he will succeed: so far as he is not this, he will fail.

We must now, therefore, consider those characteristics and elements of a true moral authority which must be found in the teacher, if the young are to be *so* disciplined by it as to grow up willing servants of the inner Law, and ultimately identify it with their own personalities as free personalities.

# LECTURE V.

## CHARACTERISTICS OF THE EXERCISE OF MORAL AUTHORITY.

THE characteristics of a true Authority make themselves known in the exercise of authority from day to day and hour to hour. It is assumed that the master always maintains the aspect and bearing of authority. This is quite compatible with kindliness and sympathy, and is always self-controlled.[1]

Summary of characteristics: —

1. The commands of the master are always in accordance with right reason. They are rational.

This does not mean that he is to convince, or try to convince, his pupils that his commands are rational; but only that in quiet moments he should be able to justify his commands to himself, or to other adults, on rational grounds. His commands must thus never be arbitrary, if they are to exhibit true authority. In other words, they must never be an utterance of his own wilful will, but have a rational justification.

2. The same commands are given in all similar circumstances. They are sure, steady, and consistent

---

[1] For an Essay on Authority in the Schoolmaster, see my book, *The Training of Teachers, and other Educational Papers.*

with themselves. The pupil always knows where to find the master, so to speak.

The master must not, therefore, allow his commands to be influenced —

(*a*) By regard for personal ease, or by indolence (selfishness).

(*b*) By variations of moods or temper (caprice).

(*c*) By personal likes or dislikes (passion).

(*d*) By indifference or frivolity — showing that he *himself* does not, at the bottom of his heart, much respect the law.

(*e*) By self-esteem or pride — showing that he places himself and his own personality above the law as more worthy than it.

(*f*) By love of popularity.

3. The master's commands are always instinct with a moral purpose.

This means that they would be found, if examined, to have a moral aim.

4. Great liberty of thought and action is consistent with the observance of law; and all things are right which do not conflict with the law.

Therefore —

The master's commands do not hover round every part of the boy's life; they do not harass him; they are few but strong, strong but few. Liberty of action, freedom of thought and life, are carefully protected within certain easily understood and well-marked limits.

5. The master's commands and requirements are clear and unmistakable.

6. The Moral Law does not require of us the impossible. The master who is a true moral authority gives no commands and imposes no tasks which cannot, with a moderate effort, be fulfilled.

By excessive exactions you justify disobedience. "Fathers, provoke not your children to wrath."

7. The Moral Law is not equally imperative in respect of all rules of conduct. The master, therefore, lets it appear that there is a distinction, and a difference of degree, in his commands; that some are truly Laws of imperative force, others mere rules or orders of expediency. There are the "bye-laws," so to speak, of the family or school.

It is well sometimes even to suspend (by way of reward) rules of expediency, when they restrict the freedom of the pupil. The very suspension enforces the distinction between the Good and the merely Expedient; and so far from weakening the sense of Law in the boy and the school, tends to strengthen it.

8. The commands and demands of the master are just.

The young are exceedingly sensitive on the subject of justice. If you are just, you strengthen the inner Law by the outward manifestation of its own all-pervading characteristics. There is much that might be said on this question of Justice, but I shall make only three remarks —

(a) The teacher's commands must apply to all equally. This does not preclude relaxations in the case of children of native weakness or sensitiveness, provided that

the other pupils recognise the existence of
the reasons for exemption, which they are
sure to do.

(b) Make very sure of your facts before you
approve or disapprove. If there be any
doubt, always give the pupil the benefit
of it.

(c) Never remember a fault against a boy when
it has been atoned for. Start afresh every
morning with a clean sheet. A new day,
a new life. Let each day be a day of
regeneration.

9. The master makes use of the feeling of awe and
reverence, which is native to every human soul, and
which finds its supreme object in the absolute all-
pervading thought of God, to strengthen the authority
of moral law; *but only in grave cases.*

If the teacher consistently exhibit the above characteristics of Moral Authority, his own personal authority, as the external conscience of the pupil, is then
justified in him: and it will be found that the pupil
will gain such trust and confidence that, should the
teacher at any time demand or command the apparently capricious or unreasonable, the pupil will
accept the command without question, as capable of
explanation and as right, simply because the teacher
requires it.

What ground have we for selecting these characteristics of the *external* moral authority? This, that
they are the characteristics of the *internal* moral
authority. It is only when Moral Law thus clothes

itself that it wears the purple, and commands the reverence of a rational being as over all supreme.

As the boy grows in years, you relax the pressure of authority as an *external* agency. You take him into moral partnership, so to speak.

# LECTURE VI.

THESE may be summed as the Approbation and Disapprobation of the educator. They are moral in their character and effect, because they appeal to native emotions of a moral, and not of a material and consequential kind.

There is so much to be said here on Disapprobation that I prefer to say nothing save to repeat the words of Herbart, that we must never so censure as to cause a boy to lose all self-respect. It is clear that blame is not felt at all unless there is self-respect to lose. The great task of the Church with the hopelessly fallen may be said to be to restore their self-respect. Approbation, again, is to be frank and generous, but with a certain reserve. You should not approve as if you were agreeably surprised that the boy should do right.

234

# LECTURE VII.

## THE MATERIAL SANCTIONS OF AUTHORITY, OR THE ENFORCEMENT OF AUTHORITY.

THESE sanctions are Rewards which *emphasise* Approbation, and Punishments which *emphasise* Disapprobation. The moment we carry material rewards and punishments farther than is necessary to emphasise the moral sanctions, we pass into the sphere of the non-moral — the purely coercive. School discipline, in its vulgar sense, always appeals to material or bodily considerations alone, and as deterrent is non-moral, if not also demoralising.

As to *Rewards.* — These are almost wholly unnecessary.

*Punishments.* — These may be classified thus : —

(1) Positive punishments: (*a*) bodily castigation, (*b*) impositions, (*c*) confinement, (*d*) expulsion.

(2) Negative or privative punishments.

A question to be considered here is the gradation of punishments. Never punish if you can attain your end without it. When you do punish, let the punishment be the minimum which will attain your end. The precise psychological effect of material punishments, such as flogging, confinement, etc., is an interesting question for the Analyst.

# LECTURE VIII.

## NATURAL AUXILIARIES OF AUTHORITY.

THE skilled teacher gets these on his side. Woe to the Headmaster who finds them against him.

They are so potent that the teacher is generally to blame when he has to resort to physical castigation. The natural auxiliaries may be summed under the following heads — (1) Sympathy of members of the school with each other; (2) *Esprit de corps;* (3) Emulation. But the chief auxiliary, without which all the ethical work of the teacher would be wholly vain, is this, that *reason is always in search of law, and rejoices in it.* Attention to the ordinary fixed rules of the family and the school, though trivial in themselves, yet promote the general habit of recognising Law.

---

The result of instruction in ends or ideas, and of discipline of Will, is, that at the end of the secondary school-period the youth is (speaking generally) a Will which has been fashioned by those set over him, and with tendencies in a definite and traditional direction. He cannot, however, be as yet said to act under a system of self-constituted ideals, *i.e.* a conscience of his own making. But he has been so wisely trained

236

that he has acquiesced willingly in ethical ideas, in the reasonableness of law and the obligation of duty, and has acquired certain moral and religious convictions. Inasmuch as there has been intelligent acquiescence, his conscience cannot be said to be imposed from without, but to be free. The effort, now weak, now strong, after conduct in harmony with his acquired ideal, continues for life.

In the case of the thinking few, however, all moral convictions and ends are, during the period of adolescence, subjected to a new and self-initiated analysis. This stage of mental growth corresponds to the university period of a man's education. Beginning with doubts and negation, it is resolved, ere long, into a self-convinced and self-directed affirmation of ethical truth, which, though it may not wholly harmonise with the tradition in which the youth has been educated, will not very far depart from it. The best work a university can do is to afford guidance to this philosophic movement of mind.

It may be said that those youths, who do *not* think, often go astray at this period of their lives, however well educated they may have been. But this straying from the right path is merely a lapse in conduct owing to the powerful impulses of nature which emerge into a feverish activity during adolescence, and not to any weakening of personal conviction as to law and duty. Allowing for certain exceptions, their recovery and restoration may be safely calculated on. There is much truth in the old Calvinistic doctrine of the "perseverance of the saints."

In conclusion, let me say that the sum of the matter is this: As the aim of intellectual instruction and discipline is to form a free rational self-activity which seeks Knowledge as Truth; so, the aim of ethical instruction and discipline is to form a free rational self-directing activity which seeks the Good as Law. These two together (and they cannot be separated) constitute the aim of Education; and if they are accompanied and sustained by a comprehension of the spiritual significance of the Truth and the Law, the Ethical End is achieved.

# PART VII.

*SCHOOL–MANAGEMENT.*

# SCHOOL-MANAGEMENT.

*Questions for Consideration and Discussion.*

WE have throughout assumed, in the preceding Course, that we have been speaking of the education of the human mind in general. But the advantages and disadvantages of congregating boys and girls for purposes of instruction and education demand special consideration. The questions to be considered are —

1. To what extent are the ends, subjects, and methods of education modified when there are large numbers to deal with?

2. What is the maximum number which should be placed under one Headmaster?

3. How many can be taught together in one class?

4. How is the difficulty of large numbers to be overcome when the pupils are of different ages and various stages of progress ? The general answer, of course, is — *By Organisation.* What do we mean by this? We mean —

(1.) *The Organisation of the Instruction.* The Instruction-scheme is presumed to have fixed regard to the educational aim of the School. · It must be devised with a view to the work, not only of successive years, but of successive terms, and even of successive weeks. Length and difficulty of daily lessons have to receive careful attention; they must be adapted to the *average* pupil.

The curriculum of instruction to be laid down for different *kinds* of schools has to be discussed with reference to the general scope and purpose of all education.

It may appear impossible to give such instruction in all the subjects enumerated under the head of Materials (p. 35) as to give an exact basis for further progress and, above all, intellectual interest in making further progress. But it is quite possible to do so, if we begin betimes and build up gradually from the foundation, falling back at every stage on previous stages and connecting the earlier with the later. We have always to think of quality rather than quantity. The actual amount to be acquired is, in truth, not great.

The difficulty which meets us in carrying out an ideal Instruction-plan is the Time-table.

The Instruction-plan compels us to consider the respective claims of the Real-naturalistic and Real-humanistic in a school curriculum. The latter is the centre round which all education must revolve.

This does not to any extent affect the position taken up in dealing with the materials of education [1] — viz. that the Real-naturalistic should run through the

---

[1] In the Class Lectures.

whole curriculum of instruction from infancy to manhood, being especially prominent up to the fifteenth
year.

Encyclopædism — its advantages and disadvantages.
Education is an extensive as well as intensive process.
Breadth of basis. Specialisation in Schools: is this
permissible? or, is it a characteristic of the University alone?

As a guide in the arrangement of the succession of
lessons daily, Bacon's words may be adapted to the
school, viz. : "Interchange of contraries with a tendency to the more benign extreme." Formal and Real
subjects should be interchanged with a tendency
towards the "more benign" Real.

(2.) *The Organisation of the Pupils, i.e.* the fitting
them into the Instruction-scheme; in other words,
Classification. In connection with Organisation of
pupils, Examinations, written and oral, Removes,
Leaving Certificates, etc. etc., have to be discussed.

In this connection, too, Class Manipulation, Place-
taking, Prizes, Expedients and Devices in Teaching, as
distinguished from Methods, demand consideration.

Thereafter, School-Rooms, School Furniture, Light
and Ventilation, Apparatus for teaching, Text-Books,
Manual Work in Schools.

In every question the Ethical End must always be
present to us, as governing all practical questions of
detail.

## Organisation of a State School System.

### *Relation of the State to the School.*

The different grades of Schools are to be determined by the periods of Mental Development. They are—

> From 3rd till 6th year, Kindergarten Schools, or Infant Asylums.
> "    6th " 8th    "    Infant Schools.
> "    8th " 15th    "    Primary Schools (Lower-Primary to 12th, Upper-Primary to 15th year [1]).
> From 15th till 18th year, Secondary or High Schools.
> Above 18th year,    Universities.

Note.—*These might be all under one roof; but in that case the line of demarcation between each would have to be strongly drawn, because each has its own idea by which its work must be governed.*

Technical Schools are schools intended to prepare for some specific industrial function, as opposed to schools whose end is purely the education of the man. The place of Technical Schools in an industrial nation. To what extent they can be so moulded as to give education as well as instruction.

Girls' Schools. — The question, "To what extent difference of sex affects the education of Girls," has to be discussed. Mixed Schools. Teaching by Women, etc.

---

[1] The Upper-Primary may belong to the Secondary Schools, and usually does.

CONTINUATION AND EVENING SCHOOLS.

THE TEACHER.

Is he an Educator or a mere retailer of so much knowledge for so much money? His true vocation, and its precise social significance as an ethical function. Intellectual and moral qualifications.

Professional training. The *general* education of the Teacher should, like that of other Professions, be in the line of the higher education of the country, but demands more breadth. His *professional* training is a matter to be determined in its details by time, place, and circumstance. (Training Colleges and Normal Schools. The Universities as Schools of Education.)

The Headmaster's relation to his Assistants, Powers and position of Assistants, etc. etc. Relation of Headmasters to Governing Bodies.

# HISTORY OF EDUCATION.

The History of education in various countries is part of the philosophy of History; for, to understand the education of a country, we must first understand its characteristics, its social system, and its ideal of human life. We thereby ascertain the standard of attainment which it places before itself, and are only then prepared intelligently to contemplate its educational machinery and methods. The History of education, adequately treated, thus contains much of those materials of culture which belong to the philosophic study of history. A day spent in an Athenian school would give us more archæological light than all the tombs.

As regards education, in its narrower sense as the education of the school, the History of education is rather to be called Comparative Education, and is very instructive. To go over the whole of so rich a field in one university course is impossible. Those portions are to be specially selected which best exhibit the progress of educational ideas, and national ideals, and also those which extend our practical acquaintance with methods of instruction and school-keeping, *e.g.* Chinese Education, Hellenic Education, Roman Edu-

cation, Church Education, and among Writers, Quintilian, Ascham, Comenius, Milton, Locke, Rousseau,
Pestalozzi.

· *The Contents of a Course.*

I. EDUCATION IN CHINA: — The home of the
Chinese and its physical characteristics.
The characteristics of their social system.
Their inner life as that may be ascertained
from their philosophy, sacred books, and
other literature. Their educational aims
and machinery. Their methods. The results of their system, morally and intellectually. Criticism of the Chinese educational
ideas and methods, and lessons to be drawn
for ourselves.

II. Following the same method we proceed to
consider briefly the EDUCATION OF THE
ANCIENT EGYPTIANS.

III. THE EDUCATION OF THE HINDUS.

IV. THE EDUCATION OF THE ANCIENT PERSIANS
— its general aim and methods in connection with their life and character in so far
as we have records.

V. History of Education among the Semitic Races
of the Mesopotamia Basin.

VI. EDUCATION AMONG THE HELLENIC RACES : —
This is to be treated in full detail. The
educational views of Plato, Xenophon, Aris-
totle, and Plutarch in this connection.

VII. EDUCATION AMONG THE ROMANS. Hellenic
influence; Cato; Cicero de Oratore.

VIII. Detailed analysis and exposition of the Insti-
tutions of Quintilian.

IX. Survey of the History of Education from
Quintilian to the time of the Reformation.
Monastery and Cathedral Schools. Rise of
Universities.

X. The Renaissance and Humanism, as represented by the literary and theological re-
vival. Erasmus and Colet, Luther and
Melanchthon. Rabelais and Montaigne.
Roger Ascham, and John Sturm of Stras-
burg. Mulcaster.

[*Jesuit Education.*]

XI. Bacon and the Inductive study of Nature: —
The rise of Realism and Utilitarianism in
Education as opposed to Humanism and
Culture. In connection with this, the advo-
cacy of "natural" methods.

XII. Analysis and exposition of the Baconians,
Ratichius and Comenius.

XIII. Milton's Educational views.

XIV. Exposition of John Locke's "Thoughts on Education," and the relevant parts of the "Essay on the Conduct of the Understanding."

XV. Rousseau, Basedow, and Campe.

XVI. Exposition of Pestalozzi and his school.

XVII. Jacotot.

XVIII. Dr. Andrew Bell and Joseph Lancaster.

XIX. Jean Paul Richter.

XX. More recent opinion, as represented by Fröbel, Diesterweg, Dr. Arnold, Herbert Spencer, and Professor Bain (contemporary Realism, so called).

# APPENDIX

ON

## CERTAIN PHILOSOPHICAL QUESTIONS SUGGESTED BY THE PRECEDING PAGES.

*A.* — PSYCHOLOGICAL BASIS.

*B.* — DUALISM, MATERIALISM (CEREBRATION, ETC.).

*C.* — BRIEF SYNTHETIC STATEMENT.

*D.* — UNITY OF REASON.

---

*May be omitted by the Student of Education.*

251

# A.—PSYCHOLOGICAL BASIS.

WHEN I say in the text that the human mind is a one self-conscious entity, I am far from meaning that it is a mere $x$ of departure for a series of phenomena. I mean that in man, as in all else, Being-universal individuates itself. This is effected in man, not only as a specific form of organic Life, but, further, of a living consciousness (or potency of consciousness) of existences which are not itself; and this consciousness, as a self-consciousness, contains in it certain activities and ends for its own fulfilment as a being or entity.

This individuated being or conscious entity is, I say, "*one:*" it is not made up of parts any more than "life" in the plant or animal is made up of parts.

Though the peculiar sensibility and activity which we call consciousness is specially allied with a specific part of body as its instrument, viz. the brain, it itself is not to be confounded with the physical conditions of its manifestation, any more than life in a plant is to be confounded with certain molecular movements in the matter of the plant.

Mind and matter act and react on each other: they are mutually involved. But matter is not mind, and mind is not matter. I stand by this dualism. To attempt to localise mind is to materialise it. It is a diffused and interfused "somewhat," whose characteristics we may feel and know; it is, as the schoolmen said, "all in the whole and all in every part."

Through *self*-consciousness I become more intimately aware of the mind-entity than I can ever be of matter.

Matter presents itself to consciousness as ultimately reducible into Space *plus* Motion. The ultimate affirmation of the monistic materialist is that Space *plus* motion in certain complexities of relation *is* mind. This is manifestly a contradiction in terms, unless we first insinuate into matter what, by our own showing, is not in its concept or notion. [What has been called Mind-stuff is matter, so far as I can see.]

Men become too much enamoured of inquiries into what they can see and weigh and measure. There is a kind of stability and certitude about such investigations. True, they find in many of the objects which yield their secrets (so far) to physical inquiries, an alien and disturbing factor. Life, feeling, consciousness, rational activity, purpose, volition, are all admittedly there before them, as certainly as the sun and moon (to say the least). Can these facts of consciousness, as sensory and active, not be reduced to simple matter-terms? If it were possible (which it is not until we alter our concept of matter), we should still feel and think and will, but we, *i.e.* that which feels and thinks and wills, and the feelings and thinkings and willings, would all alike be matter and its motions; and, thus, the morbid desire for a monistic view of experience would be gratified. If such phenomena were only matter and its motions, it is manifest that they would then be subject to the laws, and characterised by the behaviour, of matter. These laws are (speaking generally) dynamical: stone and iron are knocked about by them, so to speak, without knowing why or whither; and "minds" would be in the same predicament, with this difference, that, to begin with, they, at first, think that they are *not* knocked about; but after being "scientifically" instructed, they *know* that they are verily knocked about. Matter, it would appear, has taken, at a certain stage of evolution, the disease of questioning itself and affirming that it is not matter, and even inventing the word "mind." It thinks it thinks; it suffers in its most perfect evolution from illusions as to its own being: it even fancies it is an Ego that *wills.* I hope I do not state the case too crudely.

It is admitted that the "mind" phenomena, even as simple states of consciousness, are different from the other known phenomena called matter. But this seems to present no difficulty to the "scientific" mind (I should say, complex of matter). Quantity *plus* quality *plus* motion, feel and think *themselves!* The atom, as the ultimate of the physical, feels and thinks, or, at least, it can, after a certain evolution, feel and think; and, consequently, feeling and thinking must always be implicitly in the atom itself. But it is always only matter: that is to say, it is always quantity *plus* motion, or, let us say, energy. We should then (accepting this view) have to say that man's mind is a combination of matter and motion, such that it feels and thinks all less complex combinations, and also itself. Such a combination must, of course, have locality (for it must have all the conditions of matter), and thus we should have mind defined as a separate or individualised *one* material organic complex, with a certain relation of feeling and knowing to other atomic and organic combinations, which are like itself in all respects save in the manner of their combination. Can it be said that our presupposition, that mind is a "one feeling entity" (not-matter), demands more from the "scientific" mind than such a conclusion does?

Accordingly, I feel that I have a good title to say that there is, within certain organic beings, a one, self-identical potency of consciousness with inner determinations, and a specific activity — an entity not matter nor caused by matter. Note, I say there *is*. It *is* or be's; consequently, it is a being, *i.e.*, entity. When I say "you are a conscious entity," I merely say "you are a conscious being :" do you doubt it ? Why so coy? When I say you are "one," do you really think you are two or twenty? Any difficulty in the apprehension of a one conscious entity arises from the illegitimate extension of the concept of matter into being and mind, even to the extent of asking, WHERE is mind localised ?

All such questions can be met by another, Where is the "life" of a plant localised — the *principium vitæ*, as it used to be called? Did you ever see it? There is, assuredly, such a phenomenal difference between a stone and a tree, that you find yourself in presence of a new fact — life. You can trace the material conditions of life; but what about life itself? So also a new fact is presented to you in the phenomenon, a conscious subject, which fact we call mind. Where is this metaphysical fiction (as some would call it)? Precisely where the life-fiction is. Again, the most intimate of all consciousnesses is Being. Can you make an image of it? And yet, Does Being not be? If not, then *what* be's? The prime condition of philosophical capacity is, it seems to me, annihilation of the material imagination, except for illustrative purposes.

Further, the conscious one entity we call the human mind is not only a self-identity, but a *permanent* self-identity or self-sameness — two questions constantly confounded. Were there only a single flash of consciousness, and then darkness and the inane, the moment of that flash would be a moment of self-identity. This self-sameness remains through all the experiences of a mind. I do not understand that this consciousness of the permanent sameness of the Subject (whatever the subject may be or not be) is questioned in these days. Fresh attempts are, doubtless, made to *explain* it — attempts which, I believe, will be for ever hopeless. The mind of a man is "for-itself," not by any sudden freak or *saltus* of nature, but just as every atom and every organic thing is "for-itself." Its peculiarity is that it is *mind*, that is to say, a potency of receiving and reflecting the rest of the world, first as a *feeling*-synthesis or collocation (synopsis), and, thereafter, as a rational or self-regulated synthesis, — containing certain determinations within itself which constitute *it* as a complex one.

The most recent attempt to explain the permanent identity of the conscious entity is that of Professor James. Unfortunately his argument is involved in some confusion,

because of his confining himself to *self*-consciousness, so that
the term used by him for manifestation of mind is "thought."
This complicates things. Hume, in using "ideas," used a
better, because more generic, word. Professor James regards
the life of consciousness under the metaphor of a "stream."
The mind is composed of *a*, *b*, *c*, *d*, etc., in succession, or
collected. If this were all there could be no identity, much
less permanent identity, as Professor James sees clearly
enough. But he says: when there is a consciousness of
the presentation *a*, there is with it a consciousness of the
Ego (which I would prefer to call in this connection the
"conscious subject"). Consequently, he does not redargue
Hume, but simply *affirms* self-identity in this form. No
one, I imagine, will care to question Professor James's way
of putting the bare fact of self-identity in each successive
consciousness. But this conscious subject has next to be
carried on from one consciousness to another, as always a
permanent same subject in the midst of incessant change,
and it is here that Professor James contributes a view of
his own.

The successive consciousnesses *b*, *c*, *d*, etc., also contain ego
or conscious subject just as *a* did, and we are aware of ego
in *b*, *c*, *d* as the same subject which appeared in *a*, because
*a* passes on *itself* with *its implicit conscious subject* to *b*, and
*c*, and *d*, which, one after the other, inherit *a* as well as its
other predecessors; and so make up a stream which is a
continuous stream. There are two things to be considered
here: there is *a*, the "state" of consciousness, and there is
the "conscious subject." Let us separate them. The state
*b* inherits and appropriates the state *a*, and consequently has
memory of it. How is this possible? As a graphic way of
talking, there can be no objection to this inheritance and
appropriation; but it affords no explanation. The state *b*,
as such, can have no possible connection with the state
*a* other than that of atomistic succession. I cannot pass
on *a* to *b* in such a way as to constitute *ab* by simply drawing up a will in *b*'s favour. There is no bridging of the

bottomless gulf, the infinite inane, between *a* and *b* which would make the memory of *a* possible. The "common sense" position that the same one subject receives, holds, and synthesises the experiences *a*, *b*, *c*, *d*, etc., is certainly an explanation; James's inheritance and appropriation of *a* by *b*, etc., is simply a figurative way of talking.

This is not all, however; for in *b* there is "conscious subject" just as there was in *a*, according to James. How, now, do I feel it to be the same conscious subject as was in *a?* Thus: *a* has executed a will, so to speak, in favour of *b*, and made *b* sole legatee of all his worldly goods, including, consequently, the "conscious subject" in *a* which conscious subject possesses these goods. Where, I would ask, does the consciousness of *continuity* come in — the continuity of subject in *a* with subject in *b*, *c*, *d*, etc.? It is not in *a*, and it is not in *b* as such, as I have shown: does it lie *between a* and *b* then? It passes on, says James, from *a* to *b*. Is this not simply another way of saying that what was in *a* continues in *b* — the common doctrine? Why, then, all this pother? Must we be "scientific" at all hazards? If there is any true *interval* between *a* and *b*, it certainly is a chasm deep enough to engulf all knowledge, and the doubt would for ever remain, whether the process whereby the dying *a* bequeathed his possessions to *b* (including in these *possessions* the ego which *possessed a!*) would hold good in the courts, and be held to be an effective transference. The ego in *b* might, after all, be an illegitimate descendant of the ego in *a*. The father of the bastard might be — who or what? If, on the other hand, the ego or subject in *a* hands itself on *without break*, what is this but the perduring continuity of ego or subject, as "common sense" holds it? This "stream" of consciousness should rather be called a corduroy road.

James either grants the continuum, and his argument is mere ingenious metaphor; superfluous as it is unsound even as a metaphor, for it may mislead the unwary. It seems to induce him even to dispense with a "thinker" in the inter-

ests of " thought," just as America might be said to have
been discovered without a discoverer. Under the influence
of this point of view, he seems to regard the " state " *a* as
playing the chief *rôle*, and as handing on the subject or ego
as in it. Why should it not be the other way round if there
is to be handing on at all? Why should not the subject or
ego in *a* hand on *it*self with *a* on its shoulders. Or is it *a*
that generates the ego? I presume Professor James prefers
*a* as the chief actor in the drama, because he wishes to
escape from that fearful thing a metaphysical entity. Is he
not here making friends with the mammon of unrighteous-
ness — the physical investigator who cannot apprehend an
entity which has not a shape *at least* as solid as a vortex
ring? Certainly a metaphysical entity is a ghost. But why
this superstitious dread of ghosts in so illuminated an age —
the age of spooks? And does he not see that all that meta-
physicians mean by entity is conceded when he admits
" I "? Hume knew better what he was about than to admit
so much.

I shall conclude by quoting, from the sober philosopher of
Common Sense, a sentence which expresses a " scientific "
phenomenal truth of more certitude than the existence of
the sun as an objective reality: " I am not thought, I am
not action, I am not feeling ; I am something ' that thinks
and acts and feels.' The self or I is permanent, and has
the *same* relation to all the succeeding thoughts, acts, and
feelings which I call mine." [1]

In fine, there is an interplay between the physical and
metaphysical in man and his brain. Consciousness affects
and effects physical conditions, and *vice versa*. But if consciousness be not the physical, nor a product of the physical,
then mind may correctly be called an entity and identity in
whatever way it may be implicated in the physical, whether
by pre-established parallelism (concomitance) or by a double
action and reaction. In short, my Ego *is* not my body,

---

[1] Reid's *Intell. Powers*, iv.

though Ego and body are mutually conditioned and conditioning.

Let me add:

I hold it for true, that if man be not a one self-identical conscious entity, having within it certain capacities, desires, emotions, and faculties (which it is the business of psychology to explain), in the fulfilment and harmonious regulation of which the Ego finds the purpose of its existence, there is not even " matter " for Ethics, much less Ethics. The only alternative seems to me to be that man is simply a cunningly devised material organism of a peculiarly sagacious kind, living for the conservation of itself and the species to which it belongs: Appetite, more or less disguised, sums him up; and spiritual ideas and ideals are only painted fictions which colour, while they conceal, gross material aims.

## B. — DUALISM, THE UNCONSCIOUS, AND CEREBRATION.

GRANT the dualism of Mind and Matter, with their mutual implications, it follows, from what we know of the former by personal experience, that we must posit mind as the *prius*, and matter as its vehicle or expression.

The two being in combination, must act and react on each other: if a molecular change is produced in the cerebrum, it must affect mind; and if mind, when it has once emerged, works out its own activities by means of nerve, these mind-originated activities, again, must make their record in the cerebrum. This being so, we should not be surprised to learn that a change might be made in the cerebrum by an outer or inner stimulus which did not then and there emerge as a consciousness, because consciousness as a one whole was too busy with some other occupation to admit of the nerve-stimulus fulfilling itself in mind. But if the scar (so to call it) in the nerve-tissue *remains*, there is no reason why it should not take other opportunities of forcing itself to the front when the original stimulus had spent itself and was withdrawn. If it be, as we opine, then we should have mere dynamical *cerebration*, which can be arrested at the threshold of consciousness and stand there waiting for an open door. This would be "unconscious cerebration," and can be conceived as going on ceaselessly in our brains as a merely dynamical process. But if any one asks us to believe in "unconscious consciousness" we decline, just as as we should decline believing in "Yes-No."

Accept, however, two planes of mind — the conscious (animal) and the self-conscious (man), and we can readily

261

admit that much may be in a man's consciousness of which he is not at all *self*-conscious ; that is to say, self-consciousness (which also has its degrees like everything else) is at so low a potency (*e.g.* in reverie) that we may call such experiences unself-conscious consciousness, or rather sub-self-consciousness. In fact, is not the greater part of each man's mental life of this sub-self-conscious kind? Is it desirable that we should be for ever sifting out and binding down our vague experiences and interrupting the beneficent inflow of gracious nature? Knowledge may be too much with us. " The time of life is short;" better to live at once, then, than to spend all our time in learning what life may be, and how to live.

In the conscious or attuitional stage the nerve-dynamical (cerebration) and the mind-dynamical would seem to be in counterpoise; in the self-conscious stage the tables are turned by the emergence of Will; and while the nerve-dynamical and the mind-dynamical still, of course, remain inter-active, they are now overpowered and regulated by the Ego as self-conscious subject, which Ego has itself been effected by the free functioning of the new phenomenon — Will — determining all to ends and to law.

It does not follow from this that mind ever operates, even in its highest self-conscious activities, independently of a physical vehicle, and, therefore, of physical conditions. The world seems to be constructed on this plan — Mind using matter and at the same time being restricted by matter. This is Dualism.

When, however, we accept the involvement of every state of consciousness with brain (as of all mind with all matter in the universe), we are not *therefore* committed to a theory that every state of consciousness even in an animal, is produced by an antecedent molecular movement of matter. That such molecular movement gives rise to states of consciousness is patent enough ; but, *vice versa*, we may hold that states of consciousness are the antecedent causes of certain molecular movements of brain. When a fox sees or smells a hound, a consciousness of a certain specific kind is set up in him by means of certain physical processes, and the running to cover for concealment is also effected through certain physical processes; but the latter were set in operation by the *consciousness* of fear. When we come to Man giving external effect after deliberation to a formed purpose under the domination of an idea, we have a series of movements or processes each one of which may be admitted to involve physical or molecular nerve-movement or disturbance; but the successive units of the process, viz. consciousness, and purpose, and will are not *caused* by these molecular movements. It is not denied that when any particular consciousness arises, it involves the nerve-tissue; and it may further be admitted, I think, that the molecular movements in the cells have a *purely material relation* to past activities in other cells and revive these activities, thus *forcing* a fresh consciousness on us to which we assign its proper place in the complex which constitutes mental life and action. But, I repeat, it does not at all follow that a consciousness *as such* does not also antecede a molecular movement and set *it* up, and also give rise by association or otherwise to other consciousnesses *as such*.

If the Dualistic conception is incorrect, monistic materialism holds the field, then Mind is nothing real; it is at best a mere glow on the surface of the material organism *suffering* a series of necessary mechanical movements : these mechanical movements constitute the sole reality. This position seems to me to be so unscientific in the face of the actual phenomena, as to be scarcely worth arguing against. If it were true, every conscious thing would find its apotheosis in being a stone in order that the purely mechanical, being in that event undisturbed by the intrusion of consciousness, the conscious thing might be safely and finally put to sleep, and rid of all illusions.

The whole question lies deeper down, and the mind of man is only a single "case." Does matter (which is only space *plus* motion) think itself, and produce the illusion of its antithesis, mind? In the cosmic whole is Mind, Thought, Reason, first or second? I do not mean first or second in time; for we have present to us matter and mind in a synthesis from the first, and always. But, given the dualism of the synthesis, is Mind logically and necessarily the *prius* of Space *plus* motion, or is it the other way about? If matter be first in the scheme of things, then not only is it first in what is called the human mind, but mind itself is non-existent, save as a series of *matter-negating* phenomena following in the wake of the fatalistic series of matter-phenomena. From beginning to end all things and minds are merely dynamical and automatic; and the term "mind" demands a new definition.

*P.S.* — "*Impressions.*" — There are some who object to the use of the words "impressions" and "reflexive" in connection with the conscious subject as such; but these words, like all words used to denote spiritual facts, are figurative. We are told also that a reflexive activity in response to impressions must impart to these impressions or recepts the "nature" of the reacting subject, and *that* even to this extent that they are *constituted* by the reacting subject. Which amounts ultimately to this, that certain pin-pricks, coming from Heaven alone knows where, give to the subject an impulse reflexively to create the object. At the same time it would not be denied that these pin-pricks give the cue to the subject, and so tell it when it is to constitute a cabbage and when a dog. This ultra-Kantism is to be justified, it would seem, by the fact that all our knowledge of the external of sense goes on "within the skull"! It does not seem to occur to these writers that the consciousness of hunger and thirst, of love and hate, of the beautiful, and of the right and the wrong, also all go on "within the skull"; and consequently all things we feel and desire and think and know must be constituted by the nature of the reacting subject. The argument, with many at least, rests on the vast number of physical processes that go on in the brain before we can be conscious of anything, as if the external "somewhat" could not tell its *true* tale to the subject because of this intervention! It would then follow that the reader of this sentence could not by possibility receive what it truly contained as it left me. Before it reaches the page there is an infinite series of physical processes; it has then to be printed and be locked in the arms of a further series of physical laws and processes before the reader begins to be the theatre of another infinite series which result in — What?—constituting a meaning for himself which is not *my* meaning.

Perhaps it is unnecessary to continue the consideration of this subject; but I would put this question to these writers, Does it not occur to you that these physical and physiological processes (brain and all) must themselves, when you come to be aware of them, also be, on your own showing, constituted by the reacting subject? If so, is it not just possible that the resultant consciousness is a *true reflex* of the pin-pricks (for you begin with a pin-pricking outer), inasmuch as the subject constitutes for itself *all the processes* as well as their resultant, and so probably knows what it is about? The universe after all may be found not to be an infinite chaos of potential pin-pricks, or, to put it otherwise, a confused jelly poured into tin moulds called minds.

## C. — BRIEF SYNTHETIC STATEMENT.

MIND-UNIVERSAL externalises itself as matter — the (to us) phenomena of recipience generally. This, however, would, if it went no farther, be an inadequate expression of Mind-universal. For Mind would have still to externalise itself as life and finally *as finite minds;* always, however, under conditions of externalisation, and, therefore, *necessarily* materialised, *i.e.* in Space, Motion, and Time, which are the fundamental forms of all externalisation — which, in short, *is* what externalisation means.

All is by infinitely small degrees; and, accordingly, to fix definitely the point at which any manifestation of the Universal differentiates itself into another is for ever impossible; and this by the very nature of sense and of the act of finite reason, as I have shown elsewhere. None the less is each thing (or movement, if you please so to call it) different from another — that which precedes from that which follows. It is only at a certain stage, that is to say, after a certain accumulation of subtle and silent differences, that finite mind, under conditions of space and time, can become aware of distinct and differentiated presentations. These are then and there received as complex totals in their complex *totality,* as "things." An egg is an egg and a chicken is a chicken, but at every stage of the process from egg to chicken there is a "thing" self-identical — a total complex in the universe of things.

It will be said that if all is mind-universal externalising itself, the very primordial atom contains mind, — *is* mind. And it is so. It is monad, not atom. By which I do not mean that mind is *attached* to atom, but that the being and

266

the determination of the material externalisation is mind dwelling in and with the atom, as it dwells in and with the universe. The dynamical, however, at this stage of the cosmic synthesis, and for long, seems to play the leading *rôle* (how we know not) until we reach the thing called conscious entity, where there is an equal reciprocation; and this reciprocity becomes, at the moment of the emergence of Will and self-consciousness, supremacy over the matter-form.

Difficult as it is to affirm the point of differentiation, we may yet venture to say that the moment at which a materialised thing *feels* is also the moment of primordial mind as a *specific mind entity.*

From mere vague feeling, which is a state of indifference in which subject and object are lost in each other, the individual mind rises to sensation in which subject and object, *i.e.* the feeling-thing and that which stimulates feeling in the thing, are separated, and the object reflexly placed outside. There is now repeated in the individual as a consciousness the duality which already constitutes the universe. What follows in the evolution of finite mind is sufficiently indicated in the preceding book.

Just as Sense finds the *a posteriori* categories in mere reflex sensation, so Reason finds all *a priori* categories in and through its own pure activity: the two together constitute the universe for the subject-self.

Matter can have no reality by itself: its reality is Mind, the sole Substance. And yet it *is externality.* If we part from this Dualism, we are driven into the arms of Monism —materialistic or spiritualistic. The rose of Monism smells sweeter under the latter name; but that is all. If All is Mind, then the dynamics of what we call "matter" and the dynamics of cerebration *are* the dynamics of *Mind*, and not merely of the externalised expression or vehicle of Mind;

for there is no externalised expression — no matter. If matter, again, *is* Mind, and all is Matter, then this is simply to say that Mind is matter. There is nothing to choose between the two positions.

In reply to the dualistic position that the universal object exists *so*, that is to say, as beënt and inreasoned matter, *because* we necessarily take it up *so* in sense and reason, it may be said that it may not after all *be* so. To which the rejoinder is, How else, since that is how we know it? We cannot *know* it otherwise. It is as futile to suggest that it is not so as to raise the question whether the thing I call a poker be not truly after all a cat. To use knowledge as a knife to cut the throat of knowledge is a kind of suicide by anticipation, a self-contradiction, which cannot effect itself. To say that we do not and cannot know save in part, is, on the other hand, tenable and true ; but this does not affect the validity of what we *do* know. But we must make sure that this last is in very truth *knowledge.*

# D.—UNITY OF REASON.

WHEN the conscious subject functions Will for purposes of knowledge and consequent conduct, it asks of the thing before it, and of all things in their relations, *what* they precisely are. The answer must ultimately be the purified record of the sensate *plus* the satisfaction of the dialectic form of the reason-movement in its specific reference to that sensate. It is this end towards which Will-reason is always striving; and to accomplish it, it has to take successive steps. It stands face to face with a synthesis *given*, and it has to understand that synthesis, to categorise it: and then only does it fulfil its purpose, which is knowledge. The rudimentary act of Percipience contains in itself the mode of procedure, for it is a separating of a one complex from other complexes, and synthesising it with the conscious subject. This process of taking things, and then the elements of things, apart, and then synthesising them, thus converting sense-synthesis or synopsis into rational synthesis, is always going on. We can imagine a rational being so endowed as to analyse and synthesise in a single flash of intuition; but if it did so, it would still have to go through the necessary steps (with whatever celerity) whereby the rational synthesis was attained. These steps are all contained in the final complex act, which alone is true knowing; but when we separate this final complex act into its constituents, the logical order of these steps becomes also a time-order; because all is in Time. As separated we call them Attuition, Discrimination, Perception, Comparison, Conception of the individual, General Conception, Reasoned or Causal ground; and these movements, with their auxiliary

269

conditions in sense, *e.g.* Imagination, Memory, and Association, constitute the substance of Rational Psychology. But
the various steps are all elements *in* or moments of the final
complex act of Reason in knowing: Reason or the rational
act is to be regarded as a One in many moments.

Not only is the unity of Reason, as a one Will-movement
in many moments towards an end, thus vindicated, but it is
seen that the idea and the ideal themselves emerge out of
reason as so conceived. What we have to render an account
of are complexes, and finally the one total complex, the universe of things. Will being, by virtue of its essential nature
a free activity, is for ever restless and for ever pushing on,
even to the transcending of the limits of Time and Space.
It is the total individual thing which it has to explain in its
whole notion, and also in the idea within the notion, this
idea being the true differentiation of the thing — at once its
essence, cause, and τέλος relatively to itself. It thus insists
on pushing on till it grasps this true *isness* of the thing, to
which, however, it can never attain even in a physical sense;
and which, if attained, would still leave for our solution the
true "isness" of that ultimate physical "isness." This true
"isness" is the *idea* and the "one" which explains the parts.
The *ideal*, again, as distinguished from the *idea*, is of the
complex; it is the perfected complex: and it is Will, as a
necessary pursuer of ends, which makes the ideal (no less
than the idea) a possible fact of consciousness, both in the
sphere of knowledge, of ethics, of æsthetics, and of education.

It would be out of place to prosecute this subject further
here. All I wish to do is to emphasise the unity of Reason
and the Reason-movement as that is brought to light by
regarding Will as root of reason and nerve of reason from
first to last; the various steps in the process which psychology
lays bare being only the logical moments of a one act, though
presenting themselves to us in a time-order, because we
exist in Time.

Further, the reason act is not only a one act in several

moments according to a certain logical order, but in each separate moment the whole reason-*form* is present, and is repeating itself. In Percipience I discriminate and isolate *a*, and synthesise it with itself in consciousness; in Concipience I isolate the parts in the conceived thing, and synthesise them as a one thing (in many); in the general concept I isolate like characters in a plurality of objects, and synthesise them in a one rational thing or entity; and this process is also the process of inductive reasoning (many in one). In deductive reasoning, again, as when I say, "That beast is ferocious; because it is a tiger; and all tigers are ferocious," I have isolated the beast before me from other objects, and synthesised it with the general concept "tiger," and all that is implicit in "tiger." In affirming the cause of an effect, I isolate particular antecedent and sequent, and synthesise them in a causal unity: the one always contains the other. The simple act of percipience of the single, with which we began, becomes, it is true, more complex as experience presses plurality more and more upon me and demands rationalisation; but that is all. Thus the central Will, whose "end" is the causal rationalisation of all experience as an ultimate one in many and many in one, behaves itself always in the same way. *Each* step is rationally grounded, from the dialectic process in simple percipience upwards; and each step is also a synthesis or judgment. [Judgment and thought-affirmation are the same: the judgment-*form* exists only when articulated into subject and predicate: when expressed in words it is a proposition.]

Even the Attuit in the animal mind is, as being a resultant *synopsis*, an anticipation of judgment — a judgment within the domain of Sensation pure and simple, which, with the advent of Reason, is transformed into a *synthesis*.

If we wish to generalise in one word the *way* or form of the reason-movement, it is to be called the Analytico-synthetic way — the search for identity in difference. The ultimate result is that Will-reason, in its necessary dialectic, insists on grasping the cosmic whole of identity in difference as a synthesis of Phenomenon and primal perduring One Reason.

As a system of Reason, however, the world is outside, and remote from, mere *feeling* in the individual subject, even in its highest attuitional form. It is only when the conscious or feeling subject evolves itself as Will moving as a dialectic process, that it becomes aware of the universe as a *reasoned* system. That reasoned system, or system of reason, is outside there all the while; but until *I* have reason, how can I see the reason in it? It is not *my* reason that reveals the reason of the universe to that universe; the function of my reason is to make explicit the reason in the universe of sensation to *me*, a self-conscious subject. Prior to the emergence of reason in Man, the universal Reason is there in things and in man's sensation of things. The man born blind cannot see light; the conscious subject cannot see Reason-universal until it grows within itself the eye of reason. And when it grows, it does not say, "Light is there because I have an eye," but rather, "I having an eye can now see the light which all the while was there." I cannot, as a matter of fact, *know* the universe except as a reasoned system; the seeming chaos of sensation, from the initial to the final act of the self-conscious subject, is necessarily gripped as a reasoned world. Finite reason itself might be briefly defined as a conscious being freely moving to the reduction of all to itself in the form of Causality; which is the Form of the initial act of Percipience and of the last act of completed knowledge.

# THE INSTITUTES OF EDUCATION:

COMPRISING A

# Rational Introduction to Psychology.

BY

## S. S. LAURIE, LL.D., F.R.S.E.,

Professor of the Institutes and History of Education, University
of Edinburgh, Author of "Metaphysica" and
"Ethica," etc.

16mo. $1.00.

---

## OTHER WORKS BY DR. LAURIE.

**OCCASIONAL ADDRESSES ON EDUCATIONAL SUB-JECTS.** 12mo. $1.25.

CONTENTS.

I. The Respective Functions in Education of Primary,
   Secondary, and University Schools.
II. Free Schooling.
III. Professorships and Lectureships on Education.
IV. Organization of the Curriculum of Secondary Schools.
V. Method Applied to the Teaching of Geography.
VI. On the Religious Education of the Young.
VII. Liberal Education in the Primary School.
VIII. Examinations: Emulation and Competition.
IX. John Milton.
X. Practical Hints on Class Management.

**LECTURES ON LANGUAGE AND THE LINGUISTIC METHOD IN THE SCHOOL.** Delivered in the University
of Cambridge. 90 cents.

Lectures which treat, with a master's hand, of language as the supreme instrument in education, and as substance of thought; of method and discipline;
of the grammar of the vernacular; of the manner of teaching foreign tongues,
Latin being taken as the type; and of language as literature. Professor Laurie
is a philosopher of acute and profound mind, and these lectures are very far
above dull disquisitions on their subject. They are philosophic, animated, and
finished expositions of principle and method which should delight and profit every
true teacher. — *Literary World.*

---

## MACMILLAN & CO.,

112 FOURTH AVENUE, NEW YORK.

1

# LECTURES ON TEACHING,

### DELIVERED IN THE UNIVERSITY OF CAMBRIDGE,

BY

## J. G. FITCH, M.A.

WITH AN INTRODUCTORY PREFACE BY

### THOMAS HUNTER, Ph.D.,

**President of the Normal College, New York.**

16mo, Cloth. $1.00.

---

**From the New England Journal of Education.**

" This is eminently the work of a man of wisdom and experience. He takes a broad and comprehensive view of the work of the teacher, and his suggestions on all topics are worthy of the most careful consideration."

**From the Saturday Review.**

" The lectures will be found most interesting, and deserve to be carefully studied, not only by persons directly concerned with instruction, but by parents who wish to be able to exercise an intelligent judgment in the choice of schools and teachers for their children. For ourselves, we could almost wish to be of school age again, to learn history and geography from some one who could teach them after the pattern set by Mr. Fitch to his audience. But perhaps Mr. Fitch's observations on the general conditions of school work are even more important than what he says on this or that branch of study."

---

## MACMILLAN & CO.,

### 112 FOURTH AVENUE, NEW YORK.

2

# WORKS ON TEACHING, ETC.

**ACLAND — Studies in Secondary Education.** Edited by
ARTHUR H. D. ACLAND, M.P., Vice-President of the Committee of the Coun-
cil on Education. With an Introduction by JAMES BRYCE, M.P. $1.75.

Interesting and suggestive statistics, both of public and private schools, are
included; also courses of study, methods of grading and classification; the needs
and defects of the existing system, with proposed improvements; and much other
matter that will give the reader a clear idea of this department of education as
developed and conducted in Great Britain up to the present time. . . . Its accuracy and authority are not to be questioned. — *Literary World.*

**ARNOLD — Higher Schools and Universities in Germany.**
By MATTHEW ARNOLD, D.C.L., LL.D. $2.00.

**—— A French Eton;** Or, Middle-Class Education and the
State. To which is added " Schools and Universities in France," being part
of a Volume on Schools and Universities, published in 1868. By MATTHEW
ARNOLD, LL.D. $1.75.

**—— Reports on Elementary Schools, 1852-1882.** By
MATTHEW ARNOLD, D.C.L., LL.D., one of Her Majesty's Inspectors of
Schools. Edited by the Right Hon. Sir FRANCIS SANDFORD, K.C.B. $1.50.

No one who is making an historical or comparative study of Education can
afford to neglect these valuable reports by the late Matthew Arnold, on schools
of all grades in England and on the Continent.

**BLAKISTON — The Teacher. Hints on School Man-**
agement. A Handbook for Managers, Teachers' Assistants, and Pupil
Teachers. By J. R. BLAKISTON, M.A. (Recommended by the London,
Birmingham, and Leicester School Boards.) 12mo. 75 cents.

Into a comparatively small book he has crowded a great deal of exceedingly
useful and sound advice. It is a plain, common-sense book, full of hints to the
teacher on the management of his school and his children. — *School Board
Chronicle.*

**CALDERWOOD — On Teaching.** By Prof. HENRY CALDER-
WOOD. New edition. 12mo. 50 cents.

For young teachers this work is of the highest value. . . . It is a book every
teacher would find helpful in their responsible work. — *New England Journal
of Education.*

Here is a book which combines merits of the highest (and alas! the rarest)
order. . . . We have rarely met with anything on the subject of teaching which
seems to us to appeal so directly, both to the teacher's head and heart, and give
him so clear an insight into the true nature of his calling. — *Monthly Journal
of Education.*

**COLBECK — Lectures on the Teaching of Modern Lan-**
guages. Delivered in the University of Cambridge. By C. COLBECK, M.A.,
Assistant Master of Harrow School. 16mo. 50 cents.

3

**COLLINS — The Study of English Literature at the** Universities. By J. CHURTON COLLINS, M.A. $1.00.

This book with its description of the conditions under which English Literature is studied at the Universities of Oxford and Cambridge, was made the text for very interesting reviews, discussing its central question of "Can English Literature be taught?" by Andrew Lang in the *Illustrated London News* and Prof. Brander Matthews, of Columbia College, in the *Educational Review*. The reviewers, it may be added, reached opposite conclusions.

The author's outline of a course for a true School of Literature in a University, with hints at methods, will interest all teachers in this department. — *Post Graduate Quarterly.*

**COMBE — Education : Its Principles and Practice, as** developed by GEORGE COMBE, Author of "The Constitution of Man." Collated and Edited by JULIUS JOLLY. 8vo. $5.00.

**COMENIUS, John Amos, Bishop of the Moravians. His** Life and Educational Works, by S. S. LAURIE, M.A., F.R.S.E., Professor of the Institutes and History of Education in the University of Edinburgh. Second edition, revised. $1.00.

The papers by Mr. Laurie . . . go at some length into the permanent services rendered to education by Comenius which may perhaps be summarized thus : he insisted that education is a natural, not an artificial process ; . . . that the mother-tongue must be brought into the schools as a subject of instruction ; . . . that sense-training is fundamental ; that geography and history should be made school subjects ; that young children should be given a special training, anticipating much of Froebel's Kindergarten system ; that knowledge must be fitted to action, and education adapted to life ; and finally, that education is for all, and not for a limited number or a favored class. In our day these positions are commonplaces. But such is their value, that we do well to pause to honor the memory of him who first made them so. — *Educational Review.*

**CRAIK — The State in its Relation to Education.** By HENRY CRAIK, M.A., LL.D. *English Citizen Series.* $1.00.

**FARRAR and POOLE — General Aims of the Teacher.** Lectures delivered in the University of Cambridge by Archdeacon FARRAR, D.D., and R. B. POOLE, B.D., Head Master of Bedford Modern School. 16mo. 40 cents.

**FEARON — School Inspection.** By D. A. FEARON, Assistant Commissioner of Endowed Schools. Third edition. 75 cents.

**FITCH — Lectures on Teaching.** Delivered in the University of Cambridge, by J. G. FITCH, M.A., Inspector of Schools. With a Preface by THOMAS HUNTER, Ph.D., of the Normal College, New York. $1.00.

Mr. Fitch's book covers so wide a field, and touches on so many burning questions, that we must be content to recommend it as the best existing *vade mecum* for the teacher. He is always sensible, always judicious, never wanting in tact ; . . . he brings to his work the ripe experience of a well-stored mind, and he possesses in a remarkable degree the art of exposition. — *Pall Mall Gazette.*

**—— Notes on American Schools and Training Colleges.** By J. G. FITCH, M.A., Assistant Commissioner to the late Endowed Schools Commission. 16mo. 60 cents.

Mr. Fitch is a wise and enthusiastic student of pedagogy, the author of some specially excellent Lectures on Teaching delivered in the University of Cambridge, and a rarely good observer of new facts. . . . The book is a treasure of clever description, shrewd comment, and instructive comparison of the English system and our own. — *Churchman.*

4

# GEIKIE — The Teaching of Geography. By ARCHIBALD
GEIKIE, F.R.S., LL.D., Director General of the Geological Surveys of the United Kingdom. 16mo. 60 cents.

Among the best possible books to fall into the hands of the teacher. — *Chicago Inter-Ocean*.

A capital little book . . . original, fresh, and, we need not add, well worth close attention. — *Independent*.

These suggestions as to principles and methods of teaching, made by one of the foremost scholars of the day in his especial department, will be of the greatest assistance to teachers in awakening an interest among their pupils in this most important branch of knowledge. We commend it most heartily. — *Churchman*.

# LAURIE — Occasional Addresses on Educational Sub-
jects. By S. S. LAURIE, M.A., LL.D., Professor of the Institutes and History of Education in the University of Edinburgh. $1.25.

# —— Lectures on Language and the Linguistic Method
in School. Delivered in the University of Cambridge by S. S. LAURIE, M.A., LL.D., Professor of the Institutes and History of Education in the University of Edinburgh. 90 cents.

Lectures which treat, with a master's hand, of language as the supreme instrument in education, and as substance of thought; of method and discipline; of the grammar of the vernacular; of the manner of teaching foreign tongues, Latin being taken as the type; and of language as literature. Professor Laurie is a philosopher of acute and profound mind, and these lectures are very far above dull disquisitions on their subject. They are philosophic, animated, and finished expositions of principle and method which should delight and profit every true teacher. — *Literary World*.

# —— The Institutes of Education; Comprising a Rational
Introduction to Psychology. By Dr. S. S. LAURIE, M.A., F.R.S.E., Professor in the University of Edinburgh. $1.00.

# LOCKE — Some Thoughts concerning Education. By
JOHN LOCKE. With Introduction and Notes by the Rev. R. H. QUICK, M.A. 90 cents.

The work before us leaves nothing to be desired. It is of convenient form and reasonable price, accurately printed, and accompanied by notes which are admirable. There is no teacher too young to find this book interesting; there is no teacher too old to find it profitable. — *School Bulletin*.

# —— On the Conduct of the Human Understanding. By
JOHN LOCKE. Edited with Introduction and Notes, by T. FOWLER, M.A. 16mo. 50 cents.

I cannot think any parent or instructor justified in neglecting to put this little treatise in the hands of a boy about the time when the reasoning powers become developed. — *Hallam*.

# MILTON — Tractate on Education. A facsimile reprint from
the Edition of 1673. Edited, with Introduction and Notes. by OSCAR BROWNING, M.A. 50 cents.

A separate reprint of Milton's famous letter to Master Samuel Hartlib was a desideratum, and we are grateful to Mr. Browning for his elegant and scholarly edition, to which is prefixed the careful *résumé* of the work given in his " History of Educational Theories." — *Journal of Education*.

5

## ROBERTS — Eighteen Years of University Extension.

By R. D. ROBERTS, M.A., D.Sc., Organizing Secretary for Lectures to the Local Examinations and Lectures Syndicate. With Map. 35 cents.

## THREE LECTURES on the Practice of Education. Delivered in the University of Cambridge. 50 cents.

*Contents:* I. On Marking, by H. W. EVE, M.A.

II. On Stimulus, by A. SIDGWICK, M.A.

III. On the Teaching of Latin Verse Composition, by E. A. ABBOTT, D.D.

Like one of Bacon's Essays, it handles those things in which the writer's life is most conversant, and it will come home to men. Like Bacon's Essays, too, it is full of apothegms. — *Journal of Education.*

## THRING — Theory and Practice of Teaching. By the Rev. EDWARD THRING, M.A. 16mo. $1.00.

We hope we have said enough to induce teachers in America to read Mr. Thring's book. They will find it a mine in which they will never dig without some substantial return, either in high inspiration or sound practical advice. Many of the hints and illustrations given are of the greatest value for the ordinary routine work of the class-room. Still more helpful will the book be found in the weapons which it furnishes to the schoolmaster wherewith to guard against his greatest danger, slavery to routine. — *Nation.*

## —— Education and School. By the same author. Second edition. 12mo. $1.75.

## WARNER — Lectures on the Growth and Means of Training the Mental Faculty. By FRANCIS WARNER, M.D., Physician to the London Hospital, Lecturer of the London Hospital College, and formerly Professor in the Royal College of Surgeons of England. 16mo. 90 cents.

A valuable little treatise on the physiological signs of mental life in children, and on the right way to observe these signs and classify pupils accordingly. . . . The book has great originality, and though somewhat clumsily put together, it should be very helpful to the teacher on a side of his work much neglected by the ordinary treatises on pedagogy. — *Literary World.*

The eminence and experience of the author, and the years of careful study he has devoted to this and kindred subjects, are a sufficient guarantee for the value of the book; but those who are fortunate enough to examine it will find their expectations more than fulfilled. . . . A great deal may be learned from these lectures, and we strongly commend them to our readers. — *Canada Educational Journal.*

It is original, thorough, systematic, and wonderfully suggestive. Every superintendent should study this book. Few works have appeared lately which treat the subject under consideration with such originality, vigor, or good sense. — *Education.*

# MACMILLAN & CO.,

## 112 FOURTH AVENUE, NEW YORK.

6

# Longer English Poems.

WITH NOTES, PHILOLOGICAL AND EXPLANATORY, AND AN
INTRODUCTION ON THE TEACHING OF ENGLISH.

Edited by J. W. HALES, M.A.,
*Late Lecturer on English Literature in King's College School, London.*

16mo. $1.10.

The notes are very full and good, and the book, edited by one of our most cultivated English scholars, is probably the best volume of selections ever made for the use of English schools. — PROFESSOR MORLEY.

The poems quoted range from Spenser's Prothalamion to Shelley's Adonais, following a chronological order, and the Notes supply a brief sketch of the life and work of each Author from whom citation is made.

---

## A HISTORY OF
# Elizabethan Literature.
### By GEORGE SAINTSBURY.

12mo, Cabinet Edition, $1.75.     Student's Edition, $1.00.

Mr. Saintsbury has produced a most useful, first-hand survey — comprehensive, compendious, and spirited — of that unique period of literary history when "all the muses still were in their prime." One knows not where else to look for so well-proportioned and well-ordered conspectus of the astonishingly varied and rich products of the teeming English mind during the century that begins with Tottel's Miscellany and the birth of Bacon, and closes with the Restoration. — M. B. ANDERSON, in *The Dial.*

---

## A HISTORY OF
# Eighteenth Century Literature.
### (1660–1780.)
### By EDMUND GOSSE, M.A.,
*Clark Lecturer in English Literature at Trinity College, Cambridge.*

12mo, Cabinet Edition, $1.75.   Student's Edition, $1.00.

Mr. Gosse's book is one for the student because of its fulness, its trustworthiness, and its thorough soundness of criticisms; and one for the general reader because of its pleasantness and interest. It is a book, indeed, not easy to put down or to part with. — OSWAULD CRAWFORD, in *London Academy.*

Mr. Gosse has in a sense preëmpted the eighteenth century. He is the most obvious person to write the history of its literature, and this attractive volume ought to be the final and standard work on his chosen theme. — *The Literary World.*

---

## MACMILLAN & CO.,
### 112 FOURTH AVENUE, NEW YORK.

# MACMILLAN'S SCHOOL LIBRARY

OF

## BOOKS SUITABLE FOR SUPPLEMENTARY READING.

*The publishers expect to include in this School Library only such of their books for the young as have already by their popularity and recognized excellence acquired the right to rank as standard reading books.*

**CHURCH — The Story of the Iliad.** By the Rev. Prof. ALFRED J. CHURCH. 50 cents.

No writer has succeeded in outrivalling Rev. A. J. Church in his stories of ancient Greek history and mythology. He has the faculty of weaving into a delightful romance the hard facts of history, or in putting into narrative form the significant incidents of the Homeric poems. Mr. Church's style is clear, distinct, and to the point. — *Boston Herald.*

**YONGE — A Book of Golden Deeds of All Times and All Lands,** Gathered and Narrated by the Author of "The Heir of Redclyffe." By CHARLOTTE M. YONGE.

"Surely it must be a wholesome contemplation," the author remarks, "to look on actions the very essence of which is such entire absorption in others that self is not so much renounced as forgotten; the object of which is not to win promotion, wealth, or success, but simple duty, mercy, and loving-kindness."

**KINGSLEY — Madam How and Lady Why.** First Lessons in Earth Lore for Children. By the Rev. CHARLES KINGSLEY, author of "Greek Heroes," "Water Babies," etc.

**PALGRAVE — The Children's Treasury of English Song.** Selected and arranged, with Notes, by FRANCIS TURNER PALGRAVE, Editor of the Golden Treasury.

**OTHER VOLUMES TO FOLLOW.**

# MACMILLAN & CO.,

**112 FOURTH AVENUE, NEW YORK.**

www.ingramcontent.com/pod-product-compliance
Lightning Source LLC
Chambersburg PA
CBHW020507270326
41926CB00008B/768